DEAR ....

I BOUGHT YOU

- ❏ A CD cost too much
- ❏ You're utterly, ridiculously stupid
- ❏ I didn't have the guts to shop lift it
- ❏ I've got no taste – and neither have you
- ❏ I know how much you need something to stuff down your pants and impress the girls
- ❏ It's a nice bright reddy-pink colour
- ❏ I felt guilty about getting you pregnant and walking out on you
- ❏ I know you can't read but thought this would be a suitable introduction
- ❏ I know you collect books with green fish on the cover
- ❏ The bar code is exactly the same as your lucky number
- ❏ I found an old book token
- ❏ I fancied the girl behind the counter and wanted to strike up a conversation with her
- ❏ I felt sorry for the authors
- ❏ I thought it was a different one
- ❏ I want to propose: Will you marry me?
- ❏ We've been having this contest to see who could buy each other the worst gift for three years now. Beat this
- ❏ I wasn't thinking
- ❏ They sold out of all the good ones

FROM ....

22 OTHER STUPID BOOKS BY THE SAME AUTHORS

- THE COMPLETE REVENGE KIT
- HOW TO BE A COMPLETE BASTARD (with Adrian Edmondson)
- HOW TO BE A COMPLETE BITCH (with Pamela Stephenson)
- THE BOOK OF REVELATIONS
- THE NAUGHTY 90s
- THE RETURN OF THE COMPLETE REVENGE KIT
- HOW TO BE A SUPERHERO
- THE BOOK OF STUPID LISTS
- HOW TO BE A REAL MAN (with Julian Clary)
- THE OFFICIAL POLITICALLY INCORRECT HANDBOOK
- BACK TO BASICS
- THE ULTIMATE REVENGE KIT
- ROY CHUBBY BROWN UNZIPPED! (with Roy Chubby Brown)
- THE OFFICE REVENGE KIT
- THE OFFICIAL POLITICALLY INCORRECT HANDBOOK – Volume 2
- ANIMAL TALES (with Rolf Harris)
- THE EXTRA-TERRESTRIAL'S GUIDE TO THE X-FILES
- THE REALLY ROUGH HOLIDAY GUIDE
- BEASTLY BEHAVIOUR (with Rolf Harris)
- THE LOVERS' REVENGE KIT
- WANNABE A SPICE GIRL?
- HOW TO MAKE A VIDEO BLOCKBUSTER (with Jeremy Beadle)

The book of utterly ridiculous Stupid lists

MIKE LEPINE

AND

MARK LEIGH

Virgin

First published in 1998 by
Virgin Publishing Ltd
332 Ladbroke Grove
London W10 5AH

A catalogue record for this book is available from the
British Library.

ISBN 0 7535 0262 3

Printed and bound by
Mackays of Chatham, Lordswood, Chatham, Kent.

Parts of this book were previously published in
The Book of Stupid Lists (1991)

Contents

22 STUPID PEOPLE WHO HELPED WITH THIS BOOK (ALONG WITH THEIR FAVOURITE WORLD WAR TWO ARMOURED FIGHTING VEHICLES)

- Peter Bennett (Jagdpanzer IV)
- Glen Cardno (Crusader III)
- Anna Cherrett (Hotchkiss H35)
- John Choopani (King Tiger)
- Chris Fordwoh (Valentine)
- Paul Forty (T34)
- Rod Green (M3 Lee/Grant)
- Mary Hatton (Matilda)
- Andrea Hatton (StuG III)
- Gage Hatton-Lepine (JS II)
- Philippa Hatton-Lepine (Panther D)
- Harrie Jagger (Chi-ha)
- Gill Landau (Sherman Firefly)
- Jonathan Landau (M7 'Priest')
- Neville Landau (Cromwell)
- Debbie Leigh (Bren Gun Carrier)
- Edith Leigh (Panzer II)
- Philip Leigh (SU85)
- Alec Lepine (Tiger I)
- Eileen Lepine (Humber MkIV Armoured Car)
- Judy Martin (Churchill Crocodile)
- Rob Shreeve (M46 Patton)

just plain stupid

 6 COLOURS THAT NOBODY KNOWS ABOUT YET

- Otch
- Gandiniparate
- Nowl
- Bul32
- Scelly
- Erisque

 10 WORDS THAT YOU DON'T OFTEN USE IN CONVERSATION WITH YOUR AUNTIE

- Brontosaurus
- Leper
- Girth
- Strangulated
- Pan-galactic
- Myxomatosis
- Grindstone
- Warlock
- Neutron
- Hymen

10 STUPID BRAND NAMES FOR CIGARETTES

- Carcinogenic King Size
- Wheezy Low Tar
- Emphysema Special Tip
- Asthmatic Filter Tip
- Low Foetal Birth Weight Full Strength
- Bronchitis Menthol
- Halitosis Extra Strong
- Cardiovascular Collapse Specials
- Big 'C' 100s
- Mucus Extra Strength

8 STUPID NICKNAMES FOR MANFRED VON RICHTOFTEN IF HIS PLANE WASN'T RED – AND HE WASN'T A BARON

- The Yellow Duke
- The Green Lord
- The Black Viscount
- The Grey Count
- The Blue Earl
- The Indigo Marquess
- The Brown Knight
- The Honourable Purple

11 STUPID THINGS THAT ARE GREEN

- The bottom traffic light
- The top traffic light if you're standing on your head
- A crème de menthe and lime cocktail
- A banana that's not at all ripe
- Your neighbour's face when you turn up in a

new Lamborghini Diablo
- The green ball in snooker
- Your TV if the colour's not adjusted properly
- A bogey and kiwi-fruit pie
- Mark Leigh's old Fiat 127
- The Incredible Hulk's willie
- Kermit's ring piece

---

 22 STUPID THINGS THAT MERMAIDS CAN'T DO

- Roller-skate
- Stand a reasonable chance of winning the hundred metres
- Walk the tightrope
- Live out of water for more than three years
- Play on the right wing for Spurs
- Go undercover for the Flying Squad
- Play two bass drums at the same time
- Have a corn plaster fitted
- Drive a manual car
- Get refused entry to the army because of flat feet
- Touch their toes
- Walk down the aisle with you
- Use two stilts
- Kick you in the nuts
- Model *Pretty Polly* tights
- Wear Hush Puppies
- The splits
- The cancan
- The goose step
- The military two step
- Fit snuggly into a pair of 501s
- Walk into a cattery and get out in one piece

3 TIMES OF THE DAY THAT SOUND A BIT RUDE

- Half past wee
- Pooh o'clock
- Eight minutes past smegma

11 LISTS YOU HATE TO COMPILE

- People you owe money to
- All the things that your wife gets in the divorce settlement
- One-night stands who might have got you pregnant
- Every single word beginning with 'L'
- Reliable character witnesses for your forthcoming trial
- People to apologise to, after last night
- Prices, part numbers and dimensions for mind-numbingly dull technical manuals that you have to design as part of your job
- All the county court judgements against you
- Things to do today
- Things you should've done today
- Eleven lists you hate to compile

14 WORDS YOU CAN MAKE RUDE – JUST BY CHANGING ONE LETTER

- Walk
- Cant
- Funk
- Bus
- Jist

- Pits
- Shot
- Tip
- Dock
- Lob
- Ripples
- Bullocks
- Skunk
- Dingpiece

 27 THINGS THAT ARE COMPLETELY USELESS

- A paper frying pan
- The Pope's reproductive system
- Most of the CDs you get free with computer magazines
- Christmas crackers
- Writing to your MP
- Prayer
- Your local council
- That slice of gherkin in your Big Mac
- That twot who served you your Big Mac
- That computer you bought eighteen months ago
- Government reassurances about BSE
- A crotchless nun's habit
- A wank mag full of pictures of industrial gas turbines
- February 1847
- Presents from aunties
- All those LPs you bought back in the 70s
- That 'saucy video' you bought at the car boot sale
- Cheap plastic carrier bags
- Phlegm
- Phlegm-flavoured confectionery

- The script for Terry Wogan's *Auntie's Bloomers*
- A dead tree shrew
- Cats that explode on impact
- Nik Kershaw's musical legacy to the nation
- That novelty shoe tree you bought from a mail-order catalogue
- Saturday shop assistants
- This book

 13 THINGS THAT REALLY ANNOY ME ABOUT MARK LEIGH, BY DEBBIE LEIGH

- He decides he can't find what he's looking for, *before* he even looks
- He always leaves the lid of the biscuit tin just resting on the top and not put back firmly
- He slurps drinks
- He sniffs *so* loudly
- He buzzes like a bee when he's nervous
- He doesn't speak into the mouthpiece when he's on the phone, making him difficult to hear
- He can't blow dry his own hair
- He scratches his bottom when he's on the phone
- He never flushes the toilet first thing in the morning and tries to put the blame on Barney aged 4$^{1}/_{2}$
- He says 'March 1' instead of 'March the first'
- He wasn't at all moved by Princess Di's death
- He's not rich, despite all these books he's written
- He made me stop this list at thirteen things

8 VERY BIG NUMBERS

- 11,743,983
- 35,448,275
- 263,667,864,292
- 100,000,005
- 489,332,926
- 998,378,410,276
- 4,863,667,901
- 53,279,051

9 VERY SMALL NUMBERS

- 1
- 3
- 2.4
- 1 2/3
- 3 3/4
- 3.2
- 2 17/18
- 1.2
- 1 2/5

17 WORDS AND PHRASES THAT MIKE LEPINE'S THREE-YEAR-OLD SON, GAGE, OFTEN USES

- Chocolate!
- Bunny rabbit
- Hurt. Kiss it better
- Snuggle
- Move, Daddy!
- Hold hands?
- Microsoft

- Again!
- Father Christmas down chimney
- Zip drive
- PC
- Ningy!
- Eyes are raining
- Video
- Television on!
- Tubby toast!
- Fuck it!

---

 11 OCCASIONS WHEN IT'S BETTER *NOT* TO BE NAKED

- Meeting your prospective in-laws for the first time
- Taking your cub-scout troop out for a ramble
- A chance encounter with HM The Queen
- Giving the Sunday sermon
- When operating a bacon slicer
- Talking to your bank manager about a business loan
- When stopped in your car by the police
- Up before the parole board
- In front of a mirror, just after finishing your Christmas dinner
- Appearing in court as a character witness for your best friend
- Anytime – if you're built like Bernard Manning

22 STUPID WAYS TO ATTEMPT TO GET INTO
THE GUINNESS BOOK OF RECORDS

- Longest duration for bashing your head against something solid and pointy
- Fastest self-circumcision
- Longest period of abstinence from the toilet
- Most painful self-inflicted wound with a corkscrew
- Loudest and longest death scream
- Greatest electrical shock ever endured
- Most police officers head butted in one evening
- Most laxatives consumed by one person
- Longest time spent buried up to the neck in fresh cow pats
- Most obscenities tattooed on your face
- Most sustained period of intercourse with a mandrill
- Largest number of different STDs suffered in one calendar month
- Most spectacular suicide attempt
- Greatest misjudgement of a bungee jump
- Most live vipers swallowed in one hour
- Highest number of lobsters deposited down underwear
- Slowest amble in the nude down Oxford Street during rush hour
- Fastest loss of life savings on the horses
- Highest number of stitches needed after wrestling a puma
- Most underendowed male
- Longest prison sentence served (unjustly)
- Most time spent listening to Peter Frampton album

10 WORDS WHICH WE'VE PRINTED UPSIDE DOWN

- Spam
- Jollity
- Invert
- Undulate
- Rinse
- Balaclava
- Cactus
- Glitch
- Persona
- Dynamic

 10 STUPID THINGS TO DO WITH SPAGHETTI

- Thatch a cottage
- Do a very lacklustre impression of Bob Marley
- Scare your partner by pretending you have tapeworm
- Attempt to climb the Matterhorn
- Attach a scone to one end, thus creating the world's first edible yo-yo!
- Indulge in very gentle games of bondage
- Try to hang yourself
- Impress the girls by pulling it out of your wallet instead of cash
- Impress the girls by pulling it out of your flies
- Wear it on your head if you suffer from male pattern baldness

WHY 'BIGGER IS BEST' IS A STUPID SAYING – 10 THINGS THAT ARE FAR BETTER SMALL

- Mortgages
- The boyfriend of that girl you're having an affair with
- The list of people you owe money to
- The list of people who want you dead
- The dog currently chasing you down the street
- The chances of you losing your job
- Credit-card bills
- Portions of a particularly offensive dessert served by your hostess at a dinner party
- Your in-tray the night before you go on holiday
- Boils at the end of your penis

 10 THINGS ABOUT MIKE LEPINE THAT IRRITATE HIS WIFE PHILIPPA

- He asks me to make him cheese on toast at midnight
- He fancies girls on television at least a decade younger than me
- He doesn't change our son's nappies
- He says he's going on the internet for half an hour and then comes downstairs three hours later
- He looses his keys, watch, crucial notebook or glasses just when it's time to catch a train
- He collects comics, videos, records and just about anything else – and fills the house up with them
- He teaches our son swear words
- He leaves the tap running in the bathroom and cigarettes in the bath

- He soaks the floor if he does the washing-up or has a bath
- He likes cheerleaders

10 THINGS WITH HOLES IN THEM

- Swiss cheese
- Doughnuts
- Pierced nipples
- The plot of *Independence Day*
- The British legal system
- Pockets
- Jesus' wrists
- Henry Moore sculptures
- Nuclear-power-plant safety procedures
- John Lennon's body

6 THINGS WHICH THERE AREN'T NAMES FOR

-
-
-
-
-
-

10 STUPID THINGS THE AUTHORS OF THIS BOOK HAVE DONE (AND THEY'RE ALL TRUE!)

- Appeared on national television wearing women's tights, swimming trunks and towels
- Flicked V signs at passengers out of a first-class

railway carriage
- Stayed up all night looking for flying saucers
- Driven to Southend one night on a whim, simply because it seemed like a good idea at the time
- Turned down the chance to write a book with a single, thirty-year-old, large-breasted actress (who shall be nameless)
- Bunked off school to eat choux buns and read DC comics
- *Rhinoceros Men from Mars* impressions along Bournemouth Promenade
- Held a 'See Who's Got the Biggest Willy Contest' in a garden shed with Pam Berg result: Mike won (Mark disagrees and says the methodology had its shortcomings)
- Held a premeditated children's birthday party in the middle of an A-level Government and Politics class
- Got married (but not to each other. Now *that* would have been even more stupid!)

---

 10 WORDS YOU WON'T FIND ANYWHERE ELSE IN THIS BOOK, EXCEPT ON THIS PAGE

- Zenith
- Aplomb
- Gala
- Misadventure
- Incognito
- Downgrade
- Tribulation
- Apocryphal
- Indiscretion
- Vociferous

home sweet home

 13 PLACES WE'LL DEFINITELY NOT BE LIVING IN THE YEAR 3000

- Manchester (it will be sixty feet under water following the great Polar Axis tilt of 2096)
- Swindon (no one wants to live there now, let alone in a thousand years' time)
- Miniaturised, in a glass jar
- On the backs of giant mutated sea turtles (the experiments were halted in 2456 when people complained of getting wet)
- Anywhere more than twenty miles off the equator (how else will we survive the Ice Age of 2783?)
- In sin – with a little grey alien homunculus
- In a three-bed semi that costs less than £68,000,000
- Wales (by the year 3000 things will be bad, but not *that* bad)
- In a home supplied by the council
- In luxury mile-high towers made of glass (the vandals will smash them)
- On the planet's surface (it won't be safe until at least the seventh millennium following fall-out from World War III)
- Jupiter (*2001* was only a book, for goodness sake)
- In a room any bigger than your current lav

10 WORDS AND PHRASES IT'S NOT ADVISABLE FOR ESTATE AGENTS TO USE IN DESCRIBING YOUR HOUSE

- 'Deceptively tiny'
- '68 miles from local shops'
- 'Hovel'
- 'Unlikely to survive another winter'
- 'Built to a remarkably low standard'
- 'An eyesore'
- 'Overlooking the abattoir'
- 'Decomposing bodies hidden under the floor-boards'
- 'No bedrooms'
- 'Shite'

12 STUPID THINGS YOU HATE GETTING FOR YOUR BIRTHDAY WHEN YOU'RE TWELVE

- Checked cardigans with brown chunky buttons
- A matching shirt and tie
- A big tube of Clearasil
- A book token
- A book
- A day out at a museum
- A sloppy wet kiss from an auntie with a spikey moustache
- Any item of clothing from Littlewoods or BHS
- A Smurf album
- Fresh fruit
- Anything that your parents wanted when they were twelve
- The exact same thing you got when you were eleven – and hated then

10 THINGS YOU SHOULDN'T DO IF YOU SUSPECT YOU HAVE A GAS LEAK

- Immediately take up fire-eating
- Call the water board
- Spontaneously combust
- Decide to sharpen all your kitchen knives on a grindstone
- Impersonate Groucho Marx by walking in a funny way and lighting up a huge Havana
- Dress up in a boy-scout uniform and rub two sticks together
- Hold an impromptu firework display
- Decide it's the perfect time to strip the old paintwork with your new blowtorch
- Call the electricity board
- Nothing

 11 STUPID THINGS TO ATTACH TO THE OUTSIDE OF YOUR HOUSE, FIFTEEN FEET UP

- Fluorescent-pink stone cladding
- Any other type of stone cladding
- A large neon sign that says 'We're away on holiday, all the doors and windows are unlocked, we're not in a neighbourhood-watch scheme and we've got an expensive Nicam stereo TV and video recorder which aren't secretly marked with our postcode'
- Your new car – just so all the neighbours can get a better look
- Your neighbours, just so they can get a better look at your new car
- A seventy-foot-tall lightning conductor attached to your metal toilet seat

- Your pet, to stop it running away
- All your furniture, by mistake
- The number '40', unless of course, you happen to live at number 40
- All your empty milk bottles, just to give the milkman a hard time
- A satellite dish

10 STUPID THINGS TO STICK ON YOUR FRIDGE DOOR, APART FROM FRIDGE MAGNETS

- An octopus
- A whole roll of sellotape, just so you could see if it was really thirty metres long
- A photograph of a disgusting circus freak likely to put you off your food
- Anything that should actually be inside the fridge, rather than on it
- A half-eaten toffee apple
- All the most valuable stamps in your collection
- A piece of chewing gum (for later on, when you're a bit peckish and nothing in the fridge will do)
- A hardened steel shackle and padlock, so you can avoid temptation
- A limpet mine
- Anti-magnetic paste, just in case an enemy tries to stick a limpet mine on to your fridge

9 EMBARRASSING QUESTIONS CHILDREN ALWAYS ASK IN FRONT OF OTHER PEOPLE

- Why did my hamster have to die?
- Why have you got those books with pictures of ladies' bosoms in them hidden under your bed?
- Why do you call Granny that 'stinking incontinent git'?
- Why does the milkman touch Mummy's bottom after you've gone to work?
- Why haven't we got a new car?
- What's a contraceptive?
- Why are there lots of video recorders in our shed?
- What are those two dogs doing?
- What are the names of Saturn's ten moons, in order?

---

12 STUPID THINGS TO BE LEFT IN A WILL

- Custody of a pet warthog called Trevor
- Custody of a pet warthog called anything else
- Enormous debts
- A wheel from a 1984 Lada Riva 1200
- A map to find hidden treasure, with the 'X' missing
- A half-chewed blue biro with all the ink congealed at one end
- Two Toffets and a Mint Imperial
- A postcard from Malaga with the stamp torn off
- The solicitor's bill
- 1p
- The deceased's treasured collection of Whigfield records
- The body

11 STUPID ADDRESSES THAT YOU WOULDN'T WANT TO HAVE

- Goebbels Grove
- Cheapo Avenue
- Condemned Crescent
- Wrong Side Of Town Drive
- Very High Crime Rate Street
- Cesspit Place
- Site For The Forthcoming Ring Road Lane
- Slum Lane
- Unbelievably High Council Tax Close
- Cardboard City
- Death Row

10 THINGS YOU WOULDN'T WANT TO HEAR FROM YOUR GRANDMOTHER

- Her death rattle
- 'Slip me your tongue, big boy!'
- 'Ta-daa! How's this for the body of an eighty-year-old woman?'
- 'When I was twenty, Adolf and I were so in love, but he left me when your father was born...'
- 'And I'm leaving every single penny of my £600,000 estate to Tiddles even though I only bought him this afternoon'
- 'As you're my favourite grandchild I decided to have your name tattooed just inside my thigh. Look...'
- 'And here's the nice lime-green sleeveless pullover with matching mittens and balaclava I've knitted for your birthday'
- 'Have you ever wondered what it feels like to

have each of your fingers pulled out of their sockets one at a time by a berserk old-age pensioner?'

- 'Guess what! James Last is in town and I've got a spare ticket for his 24-hour Big Band-a-thon!'
- 'Cooooeeeee! It's time for you to change my surgical stockings. I hope my boil hasn't burst again'

---

 10 THINGS YOU WOULDN'T WANT TO RECEIVE IN THE POST

- Any note made up from letters cut out of old newspapers
- Anything from a solicitor
- Anything from the Inland Revenue that doesn't mention the word 'rebate' in it
- Your loved one's head, giftwrapped
- A reply to your lonely-hearts ad beginning 'I'm out on parole...'
- Anything that smells of plastic explosive
- A letter that starts 'Following the reintroduction of National Service...'
- A letter from your partner's secret lover, that you open by mistake
- A letter from your parents saying that you were, in fact, adopted
- Photographs of you and a domestic pet caught in a very compromising position, with an anonymous note demanding £30,000 or the negatives will be sent to the press, the RSPCA and *Robinson's Jam*

12 THINGS THAT TODDLERS HAVE AN UNCANNY ABILITY TO DO

- Wake up from a deep, deep sleep just ninety seconds after you finally get to bed
- Cry for one minute longer than you can possibly tolerate
- Pooh themselves in a big way, thirty seconds after you've struggled to change their nappy
- Forget to walk, speak or generally act cute as soon as your friends or relatives are watching
- Scream their lungs out as soon as your car gets caught in a stationary motorway traffic jam
- Lose all pangs of hunger as soon as you've slaved over preparing their 'favourite' dinner
- Hide your keys in a completely different (and equally inaccessible) place each time
- Spurn expensive and impressive toys in favour of a cornflake packet and two yoghurt pots
- Find the only biro without a cap when your back's turned for eight seconds
- Always manage to find one of your eyes when playing with a blunt instrument
- Throw up only on clothes that have to be dry-cleaned
- Develop mysterious bruises and other inexplicable marks on their skin ten minutes before the health visitor turns up

23 STUPID THINGS YOUR PARENTS SAY TO YOU WHEN YOU'RE YOUNG

- Don't do that: you'll go blind
- Stop picking it: you'll get a hole there
- It'll put hairs on your chest

- I'll tell you when you're older
- Ask your mother
- Let the air get to it
- Don't leave it, there are starving children in Africa
- You treat this house like a hotel
- Have you done your homework?
- Wait 'til your father gets home
- Don't spend it all at once
- When was the last time you had a bath?
- Call that music?
- Don't rock the chair – you'll loosen the joints
- Don't read at the table
- Don't open the door: there's a cake in the oven
- Don't play with your food
- ...Because I say so
- You wait 'til I get you home
- Santa won't come if you're not asleep
- Have you cleaned your teeth?
- Have you cleaned your hands?
- Don't say that dear: it's not nice

 20 STUPID THINGS YOU'RE SCARED OF WHEN YOU'RE A KID

- Being separated from your mummy and daddy in a huge department store
- Brussel sprouts
- Your winkie disappearing down the plughole when the bath water runs out
- Parents' evening at school
- The bogeyman under the bed
- The bogeyman under the stairs
- The bogeyman in the shed
- The old lady that lives in the corner house who

looks like a witch
- Bigger kids
- The Daleks
- Being sent to boarding school
- The dark
- Your mummy telling your daddy that you were very naughty, when he comes home from work
- What your daddy will do after your mummy has told him that you were very naughty
- The monsters in *Carry On Screaming*
- The rubber dinosaurs in *One Million Years BC*
- Mummy throwing all your comics away
- Going to the big boy's school
- The school medical and in particular the 'coughing' test
- Big dogs jumping up at you

12 STUPID THINGS CHILDREN ALWAYS BRING HOME FROM SCHOOL WITH THEM

- Crappy models made from cereal packets and toilet rolls that you have to go into raptures about
- Crazes for nasty, over-priced electronic Japanese toys
- The F word
- Their lunch boxes, minus the lid
- Strange ideas about human reproduction
- All-too-correct ideas about human reproduction
- Invitations to parents' evenings three months late
- Requests for copious amounts of cash
- Scabby, blood-encrusted knees which they want you to kiss better...
- Friends who pick their nose and then cry until

they're taken home
- Somebody else's gym kit that stinks of Germolene
- Infections

---

10 THINGS YOU WOULDN'T WANT TO FIND ON YOUR DOORSTEP AT MIDNIGHT

- Your ex-girlfriend, cradling a newborn baby in her arms
- A circus clown carrying a carving knife
- Two tons of fresh pig manure
- The pilots of missing Flight 19, each carrying a bouquet of fresh roses
- A naked Maori with a glazed expression
- Four nuns having a slash and giggling
- A midget with a wonky eye and a cutthroat razor
- Two midgets with wonky eyes and two cut-throat razors
- A long-dead (and particularly whiffy) relative
- A wreath with your name on it

---

10 STUPID THINGS TO RUN UP BEHIND YOUR GRANDDAD AND YELL

- Die, pig-dog *Englischer* soldier!
- Give us all your cash, old man!
- Granddad! Quick! Your buttocks are on fire!
- Rhinoceros! Rhinoceros!
- Stuka attack! Down, boys! Down!
- Granddad! It's the hospital on the phone...they want your pacemaker back
- Granddad! Granddad! Your catheter's leaking!

- The doctor called. He said you'll be stone dead by Wednesday
- Granny's dead!
- BOO!

12 STUPID THINGS TO TAKE INTO THE BATH WITH YOU

- A plugged-in three-bar electric heater
- A school of barracuda
- A surfboard
- Quick-setting cement
- Cat-wee-scented foam-bath lotion
- A festering, dead wildebeest
- A speedboat
- Four boy scouts and a Polaroid camera
- 40 lbs of instant potato mix and a whisk
- Someone on the 'Care In The Community' scheme and his harpoon gun
- A deep-sea diver's outfit
- Your clothes

12 STUPID THINGS TO BUY FOR A BLIND RELATIVE

- A ticket to a *son et lumière* show
- A jigsaw puzzle
- A Charlie Chaplin video
- A ticket to see Marcel Marceau in cabaret
- A pair of binoculars
- A monocular
- A car
- A shaving mirror
- A porno mag

- A white stick with a castor stuck on the end
- A stick which they think is white
- A Sony Playstation

---

10 THINGS YOU DON'T WANT TO LIVE NEXT DOOR TO

- The world's only outdoor urine storage vat
- Millwall football club
- A free-range cobra farm
- The place where the army tests the calibration on its new howitzers
- A halfway house for burglars and arsonists trying to go straight
- Mount Etna
- A graveyard full of tormented souls
- The EC ear-wax mountain
- A Semtex factory
- Sellafield

---

14 THINGS YOU WOULDN'T WANT TO SEE IN YOUR FRONT GARDEN

- 3 dogs shagging
- A crashed UFO
- A squat established by 21 Hell's Angels who haven't washed since Barry Sheen was world champion
- The corpse of your dead hamster Joey, risen from the grave
- A sign saying 'Compulsorily Purchased'
- Someone who's just escaped from an asylum, smiling and brandishing a meat cleaver
- NATO exercises

- An unexploded WWII doodlebug, ticking
- Eight-inch mutant killer slugs
- A huge heap of glowing toxic waste
- A slowly widening chasm
- An out-of-control Euro-juggernaut slewing towards your bay windows
- Most of your roof
- Your wife dancing stark naked, yelling 'Yoo hoo! Neighbours! Look at me!'

---

 14 STUPID THINGS TO SAY WHEN YOUR CHILD ASKS 'WHAT DID YOU DO IN THE WAR, DADDY?'

- I was a traitor who spied for the enemy
- Gunned down 200 innocent civilians. It was bloody brilliant
- Tortured anyone I could get my hands on
- Shat myself
- Shot myself
- Hid under a bed in Canada
- I 'serviced' Monty, lad
- Peeled 600,000 lbs of potatoes
- Went AWOL for two years
- Dressed as a woman to avoid conscription
- Dressed as a woman for the entertainment and sexual gratification of my regiment
- Killed 317 of my own men by accident
- Killed 317 of my own men on purpose
- Flew alongside Adolf Galland. God, he was a fine squadron leader with muscular thighs

11 STUPID THINGS CHILDREN SAY WHEN THEY'RE IN THE BACK OF YOUR CAR

- I want to go home
- I don't want to go home
- Are we nearly there yet?
- I want to be sick
- I want to go wee-wee
- I've just been sick
- I've just done a wee-wee
- Can I sit in the front?
- I'm hungry
- I'm thirsty
- Wheeeeee! Big Jobs!

15 STUPID COMMENTS THAT YOUR GRANDFATHER ALWAYS COMES OUT WITH

- Call this art? My four-year-old granddaughter could do better...
- Don't call them animals! Animals don't behave like that...
- And you could still get change from a shilling...
- The Queen does a bloody good job. I wouldn't have her job...
- People have no respect these days...
- Whatever happened to tunes you could whistle...
- They don't even look like motor cars nowadays...
- In my day that was a month's wages
- Shoot the lot of 'em!
- They don't build them like they used to...
- I didn't fight in the war so you could have a haircut like that!

- Here's two bob. Don't spend it all at once, lad
- Kids today don't know when they're well off
- All you get on TV these days is sex and violence...
- I remember when... (blah, blah, blah, blah)

---

 10 STUPID THINGS TO ATTEMPT WITH A FLYMO

- Conversation
- A Mike Tyson haircut
- Ritual circumcision
- Solving the Palestinian question
- Pubic topiary
- A game of chess
- Manned flight
- Thought transference
- Sexual relations
- The forging of a brave new world

---

 12 THINGS SIR RANULPH FIENNES WOULD ALMOST CERTAINLY FIND IF HE LED AN EXPEDITION DOWN THE BACK OF YOUR SOFA

- Stale salted peanuts
- Several cwt of fluff
- A leaky biro
- One of those thin yellow toffees from a box of Quality Street
- A two-pence piece
- The contraceptive pill you're sure you took yesterday
- A sock
- A crumpled-up Heineken can from the last

party you had
- The lost remote control for the TV set
- The dog's chew bone
- Your missing house keys
- Something unidentifiable but very sticky

---

14 SURNAMES YOU DON'T WANT TO BE BORN WITH

- Pratt
- Boggs
- Widdlecombe-Bottomley
- Crapper
- Wanklin
- Cnut
- Shatz
- Stroker
- Spunkmeyer
- Gay
- Fish
- Wazzock
- Tweazlegrunter
- Hitler

---

12 THINGS IT WOULD BE STUPID TO SAY TO SOMEONE WHO'S THINKING OF BUYING YOUR HOUSE

- Excuse the mess: the parapsychologists have only just left
- How we laughed when we heard that Dennis Nilsen was the previous owner!
- I hear the mortgage rate's going up by 16% soon

- Tell you what – it's yours for a tenner
- Rats? Good heavens no. It's far too damp for rats
- After the seventh break-in, we decided that enough was enough
- Now you mention it, yes, that new relief road is coming through the back garden
- That? Oh we think that's a bloodstain
- The Hell's Angels next door are really very friendly when you get to know them
- Try not to lean against that wall if you can help it
- There's one down the road just like this, but with an extra bedroom, for thirty grand less
- Piss off

 ## 10 STUPID AND HEARTLESS THINGS TO PUT IN YOUR CHILD'S STOCKING AT CHRISTMAS

- Nothing
- Last year's presents
- Last year's presents all smashed up
- A rusty mantrap
- The child, head first
- The family cat on a skewer
- The contents of your wheelie bin
- The contents of your colon
- Yourself, disguised as the rampaging, throat-slitting, totally evil bogeyman…
- A note of abuse from Santa

10 STUPID THINGS TO BUY FOR A DEAF RELATIVE

- A copy of *What Hi Fi?* magazine
- A large ornamental ear trumpet
- A talking parrot
- The new M People album
- A cordless phone
- A doorbell that plays 28 different chimes
- A cassette of Ian Ogilvy reading *The Day of the Jackal*
- A guide dog
- A radio alarm clock
- A balloon to fix to their bottom so they can tell if they fart

10 THINGS YOUR CHILDREN ALWAYS TELL YOU WHEN IT'S TOO LATE

- Mum, it's cookery today. I've got to bring in a pound of flour, four ounces of raisins, two eggs and a bottle of vanilla essence
- Mum, I'm in the school play this afternoon. I'm a Hebrew onlooker. Can you make me a costume, please?
- Mum, it's cross-country today. Have you washed my kit?
- Mum, it's harvest festival in assembly today and I need lots of tins and biscuits and bread and jam and cereals to give to the old people
- Mum, it's open evening tonight. Do you want to come?
- Mum, I've put my name down for the school trip to Russia. Can I have £150 for the deposit today, please?

- Mum, it's swimming today and I've lost my trunks
- Mum, Mrs Jones is leaving today and I have to get her a card and a present...
- Mum, it's crafts today and I need a ball of green wool, a ball of red wool and two number-five needles
- Mum, it's Show and Tell today and I've got to bring in a book about Oliver Cromwell...

12 STUPID HYPHENATED WORDS YOU TEACH YOUR CHILDREN TO SAY

- Woof-Woof
- Broom-Broom
- Wee-Wee
- Da-Da
- Ma-Ma
- Beddy-Bytes
- Night-Night
- Gee-Gee
- Poo-Poo
- Chuff-Chuffs
- Moo-Cows
- Baa-Lamb

love, sex AND marriage

---

 11 STUPID CONTRACEPTIVE DEVICES BASED ON FRUIT

- The morning-after satsuma
- Low-oestrogen mango
- A rubber pineapple
- Plum IUD
- Spermicidal grape
- The male apricot
- Loganberry diaphragm
- Grapefruit implants
- Lychee femidom
- Lemon sheath
- Cantaloupe vasectomy

---

 19 STUPID THINGS TO PUT IN A LONELY-HEARTS AD IF YOU'RE A WOMAN

- 28AA
- Jealous boyfriend

- Goofy
- Huge
- Sex change
- Hairy
- Cuddly
- Methadone dependant
- Money grabbing
- Seven children
- Warty
- Discharge
- Octogenarian
- Cellulite City
- Frigid
- Leprous
- Keith Chegwin lookalike
- Ginger
- Intelligent

---

 9 STUPID CRAVINGS TO HAVE WHILE PREGNANT

- D-reg Skodas
- Used toilet tissue
- Live goldfish on toast
- Having a biro poked in your eye by a dwarf wearing a blue cape
- A long, drawn out, messy divorce
- Photographs of burns victims
- Sixty cigarettes a day
- A stormy sex session with eight complete strangers
- Participating in an all-woman kick-boxing championship

11 STUPID THOUGHTS TO HAVE WHILE LOVEMAKING WHICH WILL HELP PREVENT PREMATURE EJACULATION

- Bernard Manning, naked on a tigerskin rug
- Bernard Manning, fully clothed on a tigerskin rug
- Armenian women
- Neville Chamberlain
- Sliding down a giant razorblade, edge on
- Flatulent Sumo wrestlers
- The EU ear-wax mountain
- Yugoslavia
- A verruca
- Motorway hedgehogs
- Plankton

10 STUPID THINGS TO PUT DOWN YOUR PANTS TO IMPRESS THE GIRLS

- Warm custard
- An ant
- An ant's nest
- Your head
- Your hand
- Another man's hand
- Concentrated sulphuric acid
- An HB pencil
- Reducing cream
- Anything infectious

8 THINGS MORE INVITING THAN SEX WITH WILLIAM HAGUE

- A plate of cat-sick hors d'oeuvres
- Having your haemorrhoids removed with a soldering iron
- A meeting with Customs and Excise
- Being a volunteer at the 'World's Largest Suppository' demonstration
- An evening with Jimmy Tarbuck
- A barium meal
- Underwear made from rusty barbed wire and leeches
- Sex with John Major

 10 STUPID SUBSTITUTES FOR A CONDOM

- Ming vase
- Packet of Swan Vestas
- Piece of tin foil
- Kermit glove puppet
- Plasticine
- Toilet roll with one end stapled shut
- Empty milk bottle
- Hollowed-out Cadbury's mini roll
- The black paper from an After Eight mint
- Handkerchief with an elastic band tied around it

 16 STUPID THINGS TO PUT IN A LONELY-HEARTS AD, IF YOU'RE A MAN

- Premature ejaculation
- Austin Allegro owner

- Destitute
- Compulsive smoker, drinker and gambler
- Transvestite
- Insurance salesman
- Acne-ridden
- Contagious
- Bi
- Truly obese
- Wife beater
- Panties
- Pervert
- Con artist
- Ex-freak-show
- Ginger

 11 STUPID CHAT-UP LINES

- Hi, I've got a small penis
- I'm unemployed with no money, no job prospects and terminal BO
- Hey, dollface, ever been for a ride in a Skoda Favorit before?
- I wonder what your head would look like on a stick
- Do you want to come back to my place to see my Hornby OO scale model railway?
- I bet you've never met someone with as many contagious sexually transmitted diseases as me
- Anyway, there I was, talking to Ian Brady when who should come into the room but my old mate Dennis Nilsen...
- Has anyone ever told you that you look just like Vanessa Feltz?
- If my friend over there said you had a beautiful body, would you hold it against him?

- So there I was, on my yacht in Monte Carlo, when...oooops!...oh shit! There I go again – filling up my incontinence pants...
- Zebra jam jar china orange balloon wheeeeeeeeeeeeeeee!!!

14 THINGS YOU DON'T WANT TO HEAR FROM THE GIRL YOU'VE JUST BROUGHT HOME WITH YOU

- I have to get up early for work tomorrow
- I suddenly feel very tired
- I like you as a friend
- I like you as a brother
- Is there a late-night shop around here that sells tampons?
- I'm a virgin and you'll have to marry me first
- Does this mean we're engaged?
- I feel like talking
- Call it women's intuition but I just know that you couldn't hope to satisfy me
- I've changed my mind
- Do me a favour and fuck off
- All that drink you've been plying me with has gone straight to my head. I'm going to be sick
- Of course the courts cleared me. They said I did it in my sleep, see...
- My last boyfriend had ten inches. I can't wait to see how you measure up

10 STUPID WAYS TO REVIVE THE NOVELTY IN YOUR SEX LIFE

- The man dresses up as Catwoman, while his lover dresses up as Pitt the Elder

- The woman spanks herself with a ping-pong bat while the man takes Polaroids
- The man smears himself with loganberry jam while the woman goes to the cinema
- The man ties himself to the ironing board while the woman pelts him with Cheesy Wotsits
- The woman sellotapes a feather duster to her bottom while her partner brings himself to orgasm with a copy of *Homes and Gardens*
- The man chews pieces of Wrigley's Juicy Fruit gum, which he then sticks to each of his partner's erogenous zones in turn
- The woman uses processed cheese slices to deviant effect, while her partner crimps her hair and recites John Hegley poetry
- Both partners sit in the cupboard under the stairs and try to identify parts of the gas meter and vacuum cleaner by touch
- The woman rubs her partner's body with an Enya CD, while the man cracks his knuckles
- The couple make love in time to Val Doonican's 'Paddy McGinty's Goat'

 10 STUPID GIFTS TO GIVE YOUR GIRLFRIEND ON VALENTINE'S DAY

- A framed, signed photograph of Ginger Spice
- A framed, signed photograph of you with your ex-girlfriend
- Some soap, extra-strong deodorant and a powerful oral-hygiene mouthwash
- A size-16 dress (when you know full well she's size 14 and very sensitive about it)
- A video entitled *Lesbo Licking Love Lust*
- Nose-hair clippers

- A £1 Woolworth's gift token
- Sexy undies
- Crabs
- A credit card

---

 11 STUPID WAYS TO FAKE ORGASM

- Bash your head repeatedly against the headboard, gasping *'je t'aime... je t'aime...'*
- Bounce off all four corners of the room, doing your best impersonation of a steam locomotive
- Say, 'Oh, I've come...' rather matter-of-factly
- Say, 'One has arrived...' in a fake, posh voice
- Run out of the room screaming, 'Yesohyesohyesohyes!!!'
- Beat your breast and yodel like Tarzan
- Roll off the bed and keep rolling over and over, whispering, 'So good...so good...'
- Vibrate violently while conjugating an irregular Latin verb
- Throw salad cream everywhere and say, 'Well, that's it...'
- Grip your partner's sexual organs as tightly as you can, pretending to be lost in the throes of rapture
- Pretend to be unconscious for such an extraordinary length of time that your partner panics and calls an ambulance

---

 2 STUPID TELLTALE SIGNS THAT A MAN'S A VIRGIN

- He says he is
- He says he isn't

11 STUPID WORDS OR PHRASES YOU WOULDN'T WANT YOUR BEST MAN TO USE IN HIS SPEECH

- Recent sex-change operation
- Three-month suspended sentence
- Biggest mistake of his life
- Syphilis
- Gay lover
- In the club
- Biggest slapper in the school
- Crap in bed
- Virgin
- I'd give them three months
- Boils

12 STUPID BRAND NAMES FOR CONDOMS

- Eensy Weensy™
- Insensitivo™
- Petite™
- Easi-Break™
- Micro™
- Splitters™
- Crappy™
- Sphincter-Safe™
- Detumescencers™
- Black Premmies™
- John-Paul Micro-lites™
- Leakies™

16 STUPID PET NAMES FOR YOUR WIFE OR GIRLFRIEND

- Whore Slave
- My Cuddly Warthog
- Dog's Breath
- Dirt Box
- Flatsie
- Fatso
- Vermin Skunk Face
- Snivelling Toad
- Conniving Bitch
- Ma Petite Cochon
- Farty
- Stinker
- Jumbo Thighs
- Thick Cow
- Haemorrhoid Features
- Frankenstein's Ringpiece

---

10 OF THE MOST STUPID ITEMS TO SET THE MOOD FOR AN INTIMATE EVENING IN

- Picture book of Vietnamese war atrocities
- Bucket of steaming cat entrails underneath a glass-topped coffee table
- Your CD of Stuka dive-bomber sound effects
- Album of press cuttings about your sex-change operation
- Wax effigy of your date with pins stuck in it
- Copy of *Silence of the Lambs* with all the good bits underlined and 'Yes!' scrawled in the margins
- Huge pentangle burned into the carpet
- Your spare false leg propped up against the

wall, near the door
- Framed photographs of your previous seventeen partners
- Framed photographs of your previous seventeen big jobs

---

 12 STUPID THINGS TO DO IF YOU WANT TO GET PREGNANT

- Run away to a convent
- Shut your partner's private parts in the door
- Keep taking the highest-oestrogen-dosage pill
- Insist on safe sex
- Date a eunuch
- Superglue your fallopian tubes shut
- Have sex within a mile of Sellafield
- Douche with industrial-strength spermicide
- Celebrate your seventieth birthday
- Say 'no'
- Stay faithful to your lesbian lover
- Have a hysterectomy

---

 11 STUPID THINGS TO SAY IF YOUR BOYFRIEND OR HUSBAND CATCHES YOU IN BED WITH A RHINOCEROS

- Oh God! I thought you were working late tonight
- It's not what you think
- Rhinoceros? What rhinoceros?
- I've been meaning to tell you about this for some time
- And, furthermore, he's Wayne and Cindy's real father!

- I just woke up and there he was
- Darling, you remember my friend Thelma, don't you...
- Let me tell you, he's ten times the mammal you'll ever be!
- It's a fair cop, he wouldn't fit in the wardrobe
- How do you like my nifty new pyjama case?
- I was feeling a bit horny...

---

 15 SONGS FOR PERVERTS

- 'Love Me, Love My Dog' by Peter Shelley
- 'Seven Little Girls Sitting In The Back Seat' by The Avons
- 'Automatic Lover' by Dee D. Jackson
- 'A Boy Named Sue' by Johnny Cash
- 'Hello Dolly' by Louis Armstrong
- 'Dress You Up' by Madonna
- 'One Night in Bangkok' by Murray Head
- 'Goodbye Sam, Hello Samantha' by Cliff Richard
- 'Hurts So Good' by Susan Cadogan
- 'Good Vibrations' by The Beach Boys
- 'Istanbul' by Frankie Vaughan
- 'Little Donkey' by Nina and Frederick
- 'Do You Really Want To Hurt Me' by Culture Club
- 'Tie Your Mother Down' by Queen
- 'Experiments With Mice' by Johnny Dankworth

10 VERY STUPID THINGS TO SAY TO YOUR WIFE WHEN SHE SUSPECTS YOU'RE HAVING AN AFFAIR

- Hello, darling. Guess what, I'm having an affair!
- Goodnight, darling. I'm just going off to sleep with my mistress
- Not tonight, darling. I only had it off at lunchtime...
- While I'm out, if someone called Sally calls, tell her I'll slip out to meet her as soon as you've gone to bed
- Slip this basque on. It looked dynamite on Lisa so it should be OK on you too...
- Darling, I've got to fly to Paris on business. Do you know where the condoms are?
- Darling, I'm just going to take the dog out for a walk. Have you seen my clean underwear?
- I just thought it was time I started wearing aftershave again, that's all...
- Sharon never complains when I ask her to do that
- Cop a load of these lovebites!

 11 STUPID WORDS AND PHRASES USED IN PORNOGRAPHIC MAGAZINES THAT NOBODY EVER USES IN REAL LIFE

- Manhood
- Porridge gun
- Swollen love bud
- 'Feed me your meat...'
- Fierce tonguing
- Plump love lips
- Mound

- Up it went for the third time...
- Nine-incher
- Love slot
- My luxury apartment

 10 STUPID WAYS TO GET ANYONE YOU EVER WANTED INTO BED WITH YOU

- (If we knew this we wouldn't bother writing this stupid book)

 12 STUPID WAYS TO LEAVE YOUR LOVER

- Via a tunnel you've secretly been digging, concealed beneath the sofa
- Out the window with an ex-NASA jet pack strapped to your back
- In a bubble car with the stereo blasting out 'Good To Be Back' by Gary Glitter
- In a wooden glider constructed from old packing cases and rafters that you've been building in the loft
- On a Space Hopper
- In a dustbin that you've been hiding in, outside her house
- On the back of a giant albatross
- Fired from a giant cannon, with a crash helmet strapped to your head
- Surreptitiously, disguised as the back-end of a pantomime horse
- In a 'whoosh' of igniting petrol
- On a brightly-coloured pogo stick
- In a coffin, after you've been shot dead by a jealous husband

19 THINGS YOU DON'T WANT YOUR GIRLFRIEND TO FIND IN YOUR FLAT

- Luscious Lucy, the blow-up doll with real hair and revolving tonsils
- *Mein Kampf*
- 25 feet of coiled rope and a ski mask
- Two packets of Ejaculex 2000 pills
- Your other girlfriend
- Those underpants you meant to wash in 1993, but kept leaving on the draining board
- A rhinoceros
- Julian Clary AND John Inman, both of whom, coincidentally and completely innocently, popped round to borrow a cup of sugar
- Your stash of hardcore mags
- Your stash of hardcore Kleenex
- That love poem you wrote to Paula Yates when you were pissed
- A large bottle of gangrene liniment
- An electric cattle prod
- That pair of saucy girl's knickers your mates have hidden in your flat for a laugh
- A photograph of Rock Hudson, signed 'Thanks for last night'
- A truss with four-inch nails banged into it
- Pages torn from a children's underwear catalogue
- A well-thumbed book entitled How To Please A Woman In Bed
- Denis Norden's Bumper Book of Chat-Up Lines

9 THINGS YOU DON'T WANT YOUR BOYFRIEND TO FIND IN YOUR FLAT

- Tickets to see the Chippendales
- A naked Chippendale
- That personal reply from Claire Rayner advising you to ditch him…and seek specialist legal (and/or medical) advice
- A well-thumbed copy of *How To Improve Your Man In Bed*
- Indisputable proof that you're sleeping with the entire population of Truro behind his back
- That photograph of you the school photographer took when you were eight and gawky
- A massive luminous vibrating stippled artificial penis
- That jumbo tube of Preparation H you keep forgetting to put away
- That picture of William Hague you've covered in lipstick kisses

14 SONGS IT WOULD BE STUPID TO HAVE PLAYED AS YOU WALK DOWN THE AISLE

- 'D.I.V.O.R.C.E'
- 'You're Having My Baby'
- 'It's All Over Now'
- 'Crying in the Chapel'
- 'Please Release Me'
- 'Who's Sorry Now?'
- 'Glad To Be Gay'
- 'Walk Away Renée'
- 'I Want To Break Free'
- 'Love Don't Live Here Anymore'
- 'So Many Women, So Little Time'

- 'We Gotta Get Out Of This Place'
- 'It's Raining Men'
- 'Gin Gan Goolie'

12 STUPID WAYS TO DISCOVER YOU'RE REALLY A PERVERT

- You're watching *Animal Hospital* – and you suddenly realise you've got an erection
- You're watching Paul Daniels – and you suddenly realise you've got an erection
- You're watching *Baywatch* – and you suddenly realise you don't have an erection
- You're sharing an intimate candlelit dinner – with an Alsatian in a tutu
- You've got more pairs of knickers than she has
- You've got 128 jars of raspberry joy jam in your kitchen
- You can't pass a traffic cone without giving in to the urge to impale yourself on it
- You check your wife's birth certificate – and discover that she's really your long lost sister
- Or the brother you never knew you had
- You go to Turkey for your holidays – and suddenly feel like you're coming home
- You accidentally pierce your scrotal sac with a soldering iron – and it feels sooooooo good
- You catch yourself flirting with vegetables

12 STUPID REASONS TO GET A 'MAIL ORDER' BRIDE

- You can pay over 36 weeks at 39p a week
- She's delivered right to your door

- You get free assembly
- You can try it on in your own home
- If you don't like her, you can return her in the original packaging within ten days for a full refund
- She comes complete with twelve month guarantee extendible to five years
- You don't have to carry her home from the shops
- If you're at work when she is delivered, the courier will conveniently leave her in your porch
- You can earn valuable points towards other items in the catalogue
- Buy two and you get a free personal stereo
- You have a 15% off coupon that has to be used by April 30th
- Because no normal woman would have you

---

 9 STUPID THINGS YOU SHOUDN'T DO IMMEDIATELY BEFORE MAKING LOVE

- Groin yourself with an iron bar
- Drink four pints of Horlicks
- Tell your partner you've just slept with her best friend
- Smear yourself from head to toe with garlic butter
- Plunge your hands and feet into a bucket of dry ice
- Read a book called *Pubic Lice – The Hidden Menace*
- Discover that 'she' is really a he – called Dave
- Look at pictures of King Dong
- Look at yourself in the mirror

Wage slaves

---

 11 STUPID THINGS FOR 'YES' MEN TO SAY

- I don't think so
- Perhaps
- Never!
- No
- No siree
- Maybe
- Negative
- I'm not sure
- Let me think about it
- Definitely not
- Not for a million pounds

---

 10 STUPID BRITISH REGIMENTS TO JOIN

- The Queen's Own Queens
- The 4th Yorkshire Quislings
- The Royal Regiment of Fast Runners
- The Durham Light Entertainers
- The King's Own Lay Down and Play Dead
  Fusiliers
- The 3rd Highland Losers
- The Royal Irish Transvestite Regiment
- The Royal Horse Interferers
- The Royal Army Hairdressing Corps
- Any other regiment, really

10 STUPID REASONS YOU KNOW YOU'RE WORKING IN AREA 51

- Half of your colleagues are grey, about four feet tall with bulging black eyes (which considerably cuts down the opportunities for an office romance)
- An office prank is likely to involve a particle accelerator or a rectal implant
- The next place along is Area 52 and the one you pass on the way in is Area 50
- There are five flying saucers in the directors' parking lot
- The annual office outing is to Zeta Reticuli
- It's so secretive you have to have a retina scan before you're allowed access to the coffee machine
- You don't take your work home with you (if you do, you're terminated with extreme prejudice)
- Friends who drop in on you unexpectedly are summarily arrested
- You don't get a reference if you leave – just a visit from two men in black
- There aren't many jobs that involve retro-engineering UFOs

 THE GIRL ALL THE OTHERS IN THE OFFICE HATE...

- Once met George Clooney
- Is a part-time model
- Wears a ring that looks like it cost more than Concorde
- Never gets a hangover

- Is naturally that colour
- Talks about work in the pub at lunchtime
- Never gets caught by the management ringing up Chatline
- Sings, whistles and/or hums on a Monday morning
- Always refers to the boss as *sir* instead of *Git Face*
- Is the centre of attention for all the men you thought had some brains

11 PROFESSIONS YOU NEVER SEE DISPLAYED ON THE SIDE OF A WHITE FORD TRANSIT VAN

- Neurosurgeon
- Poet Laureate
- Piano tuner
- Philosopher
- Cordon bleu chef
- Papal envoy
- Art critic
- Fung Shui consultant
- Ambassador
- Test pilot
- Monkey strangler

10 STUPID AND HEARTLESS RUMOURS TO SPREAD AT SOMEONE'S LEAVING PARTY

- She was caught with her hand in the till
- She was caught with her hand in the sales director's underpants
- She was caught with her hand in her own underpants.

- She wants to move on to a firm where her reputation won't stand in the way of her promotion prospects.
- The boss found out she was moonlighting as a strip-o-gram girl in her tea break
- She's pregnant
- Cosmetic surgery on that scale can take months...
- Some people in high places took offence at all those love bites
- She's going to live on a commune with some very strange American women
- She thinks she's too good for us

---

 10 THINGS WHICH WILL NOT HELP YOUR CAREER PROSPECTS

- Chronic BO
- Slaughtering your company's best customers in a satanic death ritual
- Headbutting the chairman
- Dressing up as a saucy French maid at the annual sales conference
- Appearing on the telly to complain about your company's lousy products
- Using kung fu on junior staff
- Being caught taking the personnel manager's wife over the office photocopier
- Crapping in the fax machine and then repeatedly trying to fax it through to your Glasgow office until forcibly restrained by security
- Pretending that you suddenly only speak Flemish
- Getting a degree

12 STUPID SALES PITCHES FOR MARKET TRADERS TO SHOUT

- 'I'm not asking 40p, I'm not asking 30p, I'm not even asking 20p. I want £8.40, take it or leave it'
- 'Come on, ladies, hurry up and piss off!'
- 'Everything's dear today, luv!'
- 'Get your salmonella poisoning here!'
- 'Get your mouldy, filthy, rotten fruit and veg here! It's disgusting!'
- 'How's this for shoddy craftsmanship, my darlings'
- 'Roll up, roll up and get ripped off!'
- 'I'm contagous but me fish is lovely!'
- 'Come on, gels! You don't see crap like this every day!'
- 'All much cheaper in the high street!'
- 'Gather round, gels, I'm going to disembowel a kitten!'
- 'Get your short change here!'

9 STUPID THINGS FOR A KAMIKAZE PILOT TO DO

- Take out a lucrative pension plan
- Make an appointment to have his hair cut next week
- Look forward to a nice dinner when he gets home
- Buy a Sasco year planner
- Book tickets for a forthcoming musical
- Buy a video that can record programmes up to fourteen days in advance
- Take his spare flying scarf in to be dry-cleaned
- Buy some Premium Bonds
- Practise

10 THINGS LOCAL COUNCILLORS ARE GOOD FOR

- Fertiliser
- Cocking things up
- Keeping Freemasonry up to strength
- Giving your town a totally baffling one-way system
- Slipping an envelope full of used tenners to
- Going on jollies to your twin town twice a year at your expense
- Increasing your council tax every year to help pay for their incompetence
- Paying you no heed whatsoever
- Going on holidays to the Caribbean courtesy of local builders
- Sending the bailiffs around to your house

1 OTHER THING THAT LOCAL COUNCILLORS ARE GOOD FOR

- Nothing

WHAT ESTATE AGENTS SAY – AND WHAT THEY REALLY MEAN

- *Internal inspection highly recommended* (Looks a state from the outside)
- *Bijou*   (No room to swing a cat)
- *Compact*   (No room to swing a mouse)
- *Wildlife garden*   (Never been weeded)
- *Lovingly restored*   (Chintzy, with purple walls)
- *Needs some attention*   (Needs some underpinning)

- *Quiet location*   (Miles from the shops)
- *Terraced*   (Unbearable noise levels)
- *Modern*   (Shoddily built with no damp course)
- *Easily maintained garden*   (Tiny)
- *In town*   (Situated near busy dual carriageway)
- *Georgian/Mock Tudor*   (Overpriced)
- *Off-street parking*   (There's an NCP a mile down the road)
- *Convenient for school*   (Next door to a borstal-type institution)
- *Convenient for shops*   (Located directly over the Akropolis Kebab shop)
- *Spacious*   (If you're used to living in a coal bunker, for example)
- *All-electric*   (Expensive to run)
- *Open plan front garden*   (Tradesmen use lawn as short cut)
- *No chain*   (Someone has died here recently)
- *Highly sought-after location*   (Lots of burglaries in the road)
- *Converted*   (Half a house for three quarters of the price)
- *Studio*   (Bedsit)
- *Outbuildings*   (Derelict shed and outside WC)
- *Prestigious new development*   (Desperate to sell)
- *Many original features*   (Dodgy plumbing, oil lamps and condensation)
- *Unusual*   (Designer was a looney)
- *Charming*   (Old)
- *Period*   (Needs £15,000 worth of repairs)
- *Family home*   (Boring and mass produced)
- *Reduced for quick sale*   (Grossly overpriced in the first place)
- *Ideal for first-time buyers*   (Small and full of faults, which you're too inexperienced to spot)
- *Must be viewed*   (Only two people have

looked at it)
- *Reduced*   (No one has looked at it)
- *Olde Worlde*   (Cesspit in garden)

---

 10 NAMES NOT TO CALL YOUR NEW COMPANY

- The Winkie Fly-By-Night Rip-Off Merchants
- The James Dean School of Motoring
- The Smeggy Bogey Wee-Wee Catering Company
- Fuck the Taxman Ltd
- VAT Swindlers Inc
- The Colwyn Bay Titanic Lusitania Mary Rose Pleasure Cruisers
- The Unlucky Financial Consultants Under a Gypsy Curse PLC
- The Don't Pay Their Bills Co Ltd
- Swizzes-R-Us
- The Hitler, Goebbels and Mosley Memorial Salt Beef Company

---

 11 JOBS IT'S UNREALISTIC TO EXPECT YOU'LL EVER HAVE

- A US Navy 'Top Gun' fighter pilot
- Prime Minister of Belgium
- Product tester for Budweiser
- Spiritual leader of the Cheyenne Indians
- Mel Gibson's double
- Captain of the Starship *Enterprise*
- Special advisor to the United Nations on confectionery matters
- A hitman for Millets

- Kim Basinger's body slave
- Robert Runcie's martial-arts instructor
- Anything that's much good, well paid or satisfying

---

9 STUPID PEOPLE TO SLEEP WITH ON YOUR WAY TO THE TOP

- The cleaner
- Anyone from dispatch
- The personnel manageress's boyfriend
- Old Jack, the commissioner
- The office cat
- Anyone due for retirement
- Anyone whose nickname is 'Syphy Bollocks'
- Anyone who is unmarried and has nothing to lose
- Anyone who doesn't work for your company

---

1 STUPID THING THAT PEOPLE WHO WORK IN ADVERTISING SHOULD NEVER TELL CLIENTS

- The truth

---

9 ITEMS OF CLOTHING IT WOULD BE RATHER STUPID TO WEAR TO WORK

- A T-shirt that says, 'Take This Job and Shove it'
- A Batman costume
- A deep-sea diver's helmet (unless you work as a deep-sea diver)
- A pair of old wellingtons...and nothing else
- A traffic warden's uniform, if you work in a

sweet shop
- Anything, if you're the warden in a nudist colony
- A Red Indian headdress and warpaint
- That distinctive suit you stole from the back of the boss's car
- A shirt that hasn't been washed since decimalisation

 10 STUPID NAMES FOR A PUB

- The Stale Pasty & Listeria
- The Pig & Breathalyser
- The Flat Beer & Firkin
- The Away Supporters' Arms
- The Gnat's Piss Inn
- The Three Empty Barrels
- The Jolly Short Measurer
- The Contagious Barman
- The Lager Lout & Brawl
- The Milk Bar

 10 STUPID SIGNS TO PUT IN YOUR SHOP WINDOW IF YOU'RE HAVING A SALE

- We're not having a sale!
- Closed!
- Everything mustn't go!
- !ELAS
- Only crap left!
- Everything twice the price!
- First few days!
- Everything must stay!
- Massive increases!
- Armadillo!

10 STUPID QUESTIONS TO ASK AT YOUR JOB INTERVIEW

- Who's that old bag in the photo on your desk?
- How much money do you keep in the safe overnight?
- When was the last time you had a bath?
- My mate works here. He says it's money for old rope. Is that right?
- How much sick leave can I take before questions get asked?
- What is the capital of Mozambique?
- Do you 'go'?
- Is that a wig?
- Is that all you're paying, you tight-fisted git?
- Do you mind if I roll a joint? I can't get through the day without one

3 PARTICULARLY STUPID WAYS TO TRY TO MAKE FRIENDS AT THE OFFICE

- Hold a 'Who is the Real Father of the Receptionist's Baby' Sweepstake:

Jim the janitor	70-1
Dean in dispatch	3-2
Mr Jones, company accountant	500-1
Richard in sales	7-1
Bob in sales	6-2
Larry in sales	5-1
Jonathan in sales	2-1
One of the decorators	5-2
The Man who services the photocopier	11-2
Mr Papadopolous from the sandwich bar	20-1

Her driving instructor	8-1
Her boyfriend, Les	9000-1

• Write a crossword for the in-house magazine:

Across

1 Sleeps with customers to obtain orders (5,5)
4 Jon in accounts, big secret. He's... (3)
7 The secretaries reckon his is the smallest (4,6)
9 Lisa's just a girl who can't say (2)
11 Liz is only going out with him for his money (3,5)
12 Cross-dresser in marketing (first name) (4)
15 Rachel lost this at 12 (9)
16 Who we hide from when we go down the pub (6,6)
18 Tnuc – anagram of what Brian calls the MD (4)
20 What Rick Harris has apparently been one short of since Korea (4)
22 Smells (surname) (9)
23 Michelle in bought ledger's favourite sex act (initials) (2)
25 Is for the chop, but doesn't know it yet (first name) (5)
28 The fattest girl in the company (5,7)
30 Says she's a natural blonde (4,5)
31 Must spend all of £25 on his suits (4,7)

Down

1 Didn't get kissed under the mistletoe at the last office party (because he's repulsive) (3,8)
2 Receives back-handers from the photocopier suppliers (surname) (8)
3 Boyfriend just left her for her younger sister (first name) (5)
4 Gave Katy in personnel gonorrhoea (6,4)
5 Has vaginal warts according to 1 across (4,7)

6 Caught masturbating in stock room and claimed to have knocked over the Tipp-Ex (3,8)

8 Has permanent PMT, according to the typing pool (surname) (6)

10 Naffest haircut in Western World (surname) (9)

11 Secretly phones her boyfriend in Australia at 11 a.m. every day (surname) (8)

12 Failed miserably to get off with 23 across on office outing (4,7)

13 Has a crush on the MD (surname) (3)

14 What Phil and Shelley do on overtime (slang) (4)

15 Our nickname for Julie (slang) (4)

17 He's using Valerie – and she's too young to see it (6,4)

19 So desperate, she's turned to a dating agency (surname) (7)

21 Says the MD's secretary looks like an iguana (4,5)

22 Urinated in the supervisor's coffee mug for a dare (first name) (4)

24 Petty-cash forms are a major work of fiction (surname) (6)

25 Two-timing Paul in goods-inwards with four down (first name) (2)

26 Hasn't lost it yet – and he's 28 (first name) (3)

27 Feeds half his work into the shredder when no one's looking (surname) (3)

29 Makes such loud noises in the Ladies that we can hear her in reception (first name) (3)

- Get hold of someone's ledger – and change all the 5s to 8s.

12 PHRASES YOU DON'T WANT TO OVERHEAR WHEN YOUR DOCTOR'S TALKING ABOUT YOU

- Two months maximum
- Two inches minimum
- I'd say 50-50, if that
- Who knows?
- Who cares?
- Below the knee
- Below the neck
- Big strap to bite on
- Impotent for the rest of his life
- Next of kin
- Isolation ward, and hurry!
- Call the circus

---

10 STUPID THINGS TO SAY TO YOUR BOSS'S WIFE AT THE XMAS PARTY

- Do you want to go outside for a quick one?
- So you're the bit on the side that he's always going on about
- God, you're ugly
- Pssst! Grab these A4 pads and biros! There's plenty more where they came from...
- Does he make you crawl about on all fours wearing a tutu and rubber gloves as well?
- I'm expecting your husband's love child
- Strip, Fatso!
- I bet it must have been a shock when your husband told you the company was going into liquidation
- I just gobbed in your drink
- Your husband is a rancid gelding

11 STUPID JOBS GUARANTEED NOT TO IMPRESS YOUR BOYFRIEND'S PARENTS

- Dominatrix
- Surrogate mother
- Vibrator tester
- Traffic warden
- Gangster's moll
- Sexologist
- Masseuse
- Trollop
- Saucy kissogram
- Professional mistress
- Female impersonator

10 JOBS YOU DON'T OFTEN SEE ADVERTISED DOWN AT YOUR LOCAL CAREERS OFFICE

- Nazi hunter
- Speaker of the House of Commons
- Atomic physicist
- Double agent
- Ranch hand
- Space-shuttle pilot
- Human guinea pig
- Pioneering brain surgeon
- Queen
- Film director

science
fictions

 11 THINGS THAT ARE HOTTER THAN YOU THINK

- Alpha Centauri
- That tip you ignored for the 3.15 at Newmarket
- Peter Bennett's kettle, just after it's boiled
- That Pyrex bowl left on the work surface
- The Blaupunkt 'Berlin' car radio that you bought from a friend for £40
- The plastic cup full of McDonald's tea that you've just spilled on your lap
- The spark plug you've just taken out for checking
- The blind date with your sister's friend that you turned down
- The police lead on you for buying that £40 car radio
- The Bangalore phal chicken curry that you thought sounded interesting
- Your bottom, after eating that Bangalore phal chicken curry

 1 FRUIT THAT LOOKS LIKE A BANANA

- Banana

10 THINGS YOU CAN'T DO VERY WELL ON THE SURFACE OF MERCURY

- Survive for more than 0.002 seconds
- Eat a raspberry Cornetto
- Levitate a bowl of fruit, just by looking at it
- Travel to Torremolinos on holiday
- Play ice hockey
- Collect train numbers
- Get Pizza Hut to deliver a Spicy Hot One
- Watch Arsenal at home
- Make a reasonable snowman
- Do an honest day's work (a Mercurian day is the equivalent to 59 Earth days)

---

10 SNEAKY METHODS OF DISPOSING OF TOXIC WASTE ABROAD

- Leave it in black plastic bin liners on the French side of the Channel Tunnel at night
- Disguise it as models of beefeaters, the Tower of London and policeman's helmets for visiting tourists to take home with them. N.B. A particularly large amount of waste would require a Royal Wedding to stimulate the additional demand for souvenirs. (It is predicted that Prince Edward's marriage would enable 1.4 million tonnes of waste disguised as commemorative plates to be disposed of)
- Add it to British wines or sherry for export (this won't affect their saleability. They all taste like crap, anyway)
- Produce an exact replica of the Elgin marbles from decaying Plutonium and agree to return them to Greece

- Get the Royal Navy to make goodwill tours to foreign ports. When it's dark they can throw it off the side of the ships
- Before they perform abroad, get the men in the Royal Ballet to fill their codpieces with waste. This can then be discreetly jettisoned after the final *pas de deux* when no one's looking
- Fill up black plastic sacks with toxic waste and write 'Diplomatic Bag' on them, then dump them abroad somewhere
- Make it into condoms and offer them free at airports (the fact that they make the wearer sterile makes them an even better contraceptive)
- Jettison it under the guise of coloured smoke trailed behind the Red Arrows display team when they're on a world tour
- Use toxic waste in the ink used to stamp foreign tourists' passports, and in airmail stickers for envelopes or postcards

 16 STUPID SUPERHEROES

- Walk-Backwards Man
- The Scarlet Procrastinator
- Captain Dead
- Upside-Down Lad
- Smell Master
- Marmite Man
- The Tickler
- Unconcious Man
- Mr Stand Still
- Vanisho, Master of Ancient Hiding Techniques
- Rude Noise King
- Captain Hopscotch

- Salad Dressing Lad
- Mr Eat-Himself
- Sex Change King/Queen
- The Tease

 9 THINGS THAT ALBERT EINSTEIN PROBABLY NEVER SAID

- Hi, dollface. My name's Al. I'm father of the atomic bomb. Can I buy you a drink?
- Yes! If this experiment succeeds I'll be able to rule the world! Ha, ha, ha, ha, ha!!!
- Look, Adolf, if the Americans don't want it I'll give you first refusal, OK?
- Sigmund, darling, we can't go on meeting like this!
- Yo! President Eisenhower! Gimme five!
- Gott und himmel! I'm pregnant!
- $e = mc^3$
- $e = mc$ hammer
- Come on then, if you think you're hard enough!

 13 STUPID REASONS TO GET ON THE INTERNET

- You enjoy receiving quarterly phone bills in excess of £500
- You don't think you're absorbing enough screen radiation from your PC at work
- Your life's ambition is to pretend to be an exotic dancer from Nevada
- You enjoy receiving 200 unsolicited e-mails a day from the likes of big.n.busty.com and oiled.cheerleaders.com

- You like staring into space for ten minutes waiting for a photograph the size of a stamp to download
- You think you can beat the odds and be the one who actually finds something using a search engine
- You don't care if the information you get is right or wrong
- You want to have fantasy virtual sex with a woman who's actually a beefy, sweaty truck driver from Arkansas
- You're looking to strike up friendships with people who are even sadder than you are
- You want your credit card to be used by a gang of juvenile Brazilian hackers
- You particularly like the 'engaged' sound that your modem makes 95% of the time
- You think that someone will be remotely interested in your web site with all those pictures of your pets
- You're not already getting enough exercise with your right hand

---

5 OTHER, MUCH RUDER ANOMALIES NASA REFUSES TO INVESTIGATE IN ADDITION TO THE 'FACE ON MARS'

- The Scrotum on Neptune
- The Bosom on Jupiter
- The Clitoris on Pluto
- The Glans on Mercury
- The Sphincter on Uranus (not to be confused with the Rings of Saturn)

10 PLANTS YOU WOULDN'T WANT TO MEET IN A DARK ALLEY

- Ellison's bushwacking marigold
- Rhododendrons hell-bent on revenge
- A delinquent foxglove
- The Shrub Gang
- A carnation that thinks it's a triffid
- A lily with a grudge
- A psychopathic dandelion
- A sweet pea desperate for its next fix of crack
- A Venus flytrap with nothing left to lose
- A privet hedge with a semi-automatic weapon

11 STUPID WAYS TO TRY TO PROVE YOUR NEW SCIENTIFIC THEORY

- Toss a coin
- Challenge all sceptics to an arm-wrestling contest
- Ask Zoë Ball what she thinks
- Say, 'It's right because it is!'
- Dissect a Member of Parliament on live television
- Say, 'My horoscope says I'll make a major scientific breakthrough this week...'
- Put your hand in a blender and switch it on
- By a combination of martial arts and crochet work
- Put your trousers over your head and chase buses down the high street
- Cite 'indisputable evidence' from articles in the *Sunday Sport*
- With a bunsen burner and a wriggly kitten

10 UNHAPPY TREES

- Weeping willows
- Distraught elms
- Inconsolable oaks
- Distressed larches
- Sobbing figs
- Manically depressed palms
- A miserable birch
- Tormented pines
- Suicidal bonsai
- Peeved firs

10 STUPID FACTS ABOUT THE SUN

- It's big
- It's yellow
- It's quite hot
- If you tried to fly there it would take a long time
- It gets in your eyes
- It doesn't really have a hat on
- It's still there, even at night (it's just that we can't see it)
- We all revolve around it
- If it wasn't there, we'd be cold
- Icarus thought he could fly there (prat)

11 STUPID INVENTIONS TO TRY TO PATENT

- A dormouse with a genetically enhanced ribcage that acts as a furry, mobile toast rack
- Cheese that goes faster than sound
- Cars that save fuel by not going

- Mail-order lizard brides
- A forty-foot soup spoon
- Pre-soiled underwear
- A sophisticated electronic device which discourages Spice Girls from getting into bed with you
- A solar calculator which adds 47.6878 to all your calculations
- Genetically altered otters which fit in your ears
- Edible homes
- Musical broccoli

8 THINGS THAT RUTHERFORD SPLIT BEFORE THE ATOM

- His lip
- The lip of his arch scientific rival
- His head open (after his arch scientific rival smacked him one)
- Infinitives
- His trousers
- His sides (at a stupid joke about relativity)
- A banana (inventing a brand-new dessert into the bargain)
- His personality

On the road

🚲 **9 METHODS OF TRANSPORTATION THAT ARE DOOMED FROM THE START**

- A team of eight lobsters harnessed to a shopping trolley
- A sedan chair carried by two itinerant orang-utans
- Piggy backs offered by anyone who fought in the Somme
- An electric double-decker bus powered by 4,900 hamsters generating current from their exercise wheels
- A white rhinoceros with a saddle on its back
- A Dayglo pink Skoda with lime-green shiny plastic upholstery powered by animal effluent and priced at £38,000
- Solar-powered anything
- Lunar-powered anything
- The Sinclair C6

🚂 **13 THINGS PEOPLE THINK TO THEMSELVES ON A CROWDED TRAIN**

- Turn that fucking Walkman off or I'll punch it down your throat
- Ha, Ha! I've got a seat and you haven't

- I wonder what he/she's like in bed
- Prat
- If she would just move her leg a bit I could see right up her skirt
- Phworrrr! Who farted?
- I wish he'd stop sniffing and blow his nose
- I wish this erection would go down
- Why do the horny girls always get into the other carriages?
- I hope that loony doesn't come anywhere near me
- Don't fancy yours, mate
- I'm going to be late
- I'm going to be very late

18 REASONS WHY CARS MADE OF CHEESE WILL NEVER CATCH ON

- Passing birds (and pecking pedestrians) would be tempted to take a bite out of them
- They'd dissolve in the car wash
- If you took one for a drive in the summer the smell would be unpleasant
- You'd feel silly putting a sign up in the rear window that said, 'My Other Cheese Is A Gouda'
- If your car caught fire, you'd have more fondue than you knew what to do with
- They'd go mouldy unless you stored them in a Tupperware garage
- You wouldn't feel very masculine driving the Ford Wensleydale
- Or the Fiat Parmesan
- Swiss cars would be very draughty
- You'd have to get your MOT from a delicatessen

- Vandals might come along in the night and grate it
- In a collision, drivers in a soft cheese wouldn't stand a chance
- Bank robbers would have little confidence in a getaway Cheddar
- Who wants to make out in the back of a Camembert?
- Murray Walker saying, 'There goes Schumacher in the Edam; he's being pressed hard by Hill in the Yarlsbourg!' would lack drama somehow
- If Steve McQueen had driven around in a Cracker Barrel in *Bullit*, the film would never have become a classic
- Even Jeremy Clarkson wouldn't be able to get sexually aroused sliding his hands down the side of a sweaty piece of Brie
- If we wanted a car that stank to high heaven we'd buy a Proton

10 THINGS IT'S NOT ADVISABLE TO DO WITH YOUR CAR

- Drive it everywhere at 60 mph in reverse
- Report it stolen, collect the insurance money and then drive it back and forth outside a police station with the horn blaring
- Pour concentrated hydrofluoric acid all over the paintwork
- Leave it outside a scrap yard with a big sign on the roof saying 'Not Wanted'
- Submerge it in a nearby canal
- Force the door lock, smash the window and rip out the stereo
- Attempt to leap over fourteen double-decker

buses parked side by side on live TV
- Drive the wrong way around the M25 about 4.30 on a Friday afternoon
- Trade it in for a P-reg Austin Allegro
- Lend it free of charge to a mini-cab company

---

13 USEFUL WAYS TO HELP IDENTIFY THE DRIVER OF A WHITE VAN

- His lips move when he reads road signs (IF he reads road signs)
- His forehead protrudes beyond his jaw
- His IQ is half that of his van's top speed (fully laden)
- His mates are called Kev, Bill, Mick, Darren and Steve
- And so are his kids
- His idea of a sophisticated, elegant, intelligent woman is Posh Spice
- He has the ability to drive while scratching his arse with one hand and giving the finger with the other
- He looks like he smells of petrol, fags and Pils
- He does
- His role models are the Mitchell brothers and Jim Davidson
- He makes mini-cab drivers seem tolerant
- He drives like he owns the road (which is ironic since he hasn't paid any road tax since 1983)
- The vehicle he drives is white – and it's a van

11 OF THE WORST DRIVERS TO GET STUCK BEHIND

- An old lady in a Morris Minor
- An old man in a Morris Minor
- An old couple in a Morris Minor
- Anyone else in a Morris Minor
- Anyone towing a caravan
- Anyone wearing a hat (especially if they're in a Morris Minor)
- Anyone in a hearse, milkfloat, tractor or steam-roller
- Anyone from abroad
- Anyone who has no prior knowledge of how to control a motor vehicle
- Anyone who's stationary
- Anyone who's suddenly decided to reverse all the way home

 ## 7 MOTORING AWARDS WON BY THE LADA SAMARA

- 1990: Outright Winner 'Car I'd Least Like To Own'
- 1991: Outright Winner 'Car I'd Still Least Like To Own'
- 1992: 'Low-Performance Car Of The Year'
- 1992: Overall Winner Of Germany's Autoschiesen Trophy
- 1993: Outright Champion 'Car I'd Least Like To Be Seen Driving'
- 1994: Auto Manufacturer's Special 'Shame On The Industry' Award
- 1996: Industrie de Mechanique Français 'Voiture Merde De L'Année'

10 STUPID THINGS YOU'LL NEVER HEAR A TAXI DRIVER SAY

- Keep the change, mate!
- Watford to Wimbledon at midnight? No problem
- Have this trip on me, darling
- Ethnic minorities? They've got as many rights as you or me, mister
- The World Cup? Couldn't give a monkeys!
- … Of course, if you want to trace the origin of modern vegetation you only have to study the plant life of the Miocene Era, guv
- Do you know who I had in the back of my cab last week? Edward VIII
- Do you mind not talking to me: I'm trying to concentrate on my driving
- Anything of consequence
- Or interest

 15 STUPID THINGS YOU SEE ON THE MOTORWAY

- Cretins driving cars
- Cretins driving vans
- Cretins driving lorries
- Miles of seemingly pointless traffic cones
- Disregard for safe braking distances
- Squashed wildlife
- A Porsche or BMW with a blonde in the passenger seat, going past you at 130 mph
- Spectacular errors of judgement
- Somewhat interesting lane discipline
- People flashing their lights at each other, making frantic V signs and mouthing obscenities

- Speeds that would make Eddie Irvine shit himself
- People taking the wrong exit, realising their mistake at the last moment and swerving back straight in front of you
- People waiting for the RAC
- The lorry in front of you shedding half its load directly in your path
- Loads of hitchhikers you don't fancy

9 THINGS YOU NEVER HEAR USED-CAR SALESMEN SAY

- Name your price
- It was previously owned by a well-known hire company
- If you look under the carpet you can see that it's been completely resprayed
- I think it's actually two different cars, both insurance write-offs, welded together
- I wouldn't trust the milometer if I were you, sir. It's probably been round the clock at least three times
- The previous owner died because the brakes failed for no apparent reason
- That little squeak? I'd say it was something major
- And we'll guarantee it against any defect for five years or 100,000 miles
- They don't all do that, sir

10 STUPID THINGS TO LOSE ON A TRAIN

- Your fight against terminal syphilis

- All hope of ever finding any survivors
- Your way
- Your mind
- Your struggle against an imperialist society
- A case containing all your ticket-forging equipment with your name and address inside it
- Your grip on reality
- All sense of direction
- Your independence
- Face

---

10 PARTS OF A CAR THAT SOUND A BIT RUDE

- Wankel engine
- Half shaft
- Piston
- Big end
- Crank
- Push rod
- Sump
- Thrust bearing
- Dip stick
- Ball joint

 ## 10 STUPID THINGS TO CALL THE RAC OUT FOR

- Clean your windscreen
- Empty the ashtray
- Remove your Lighthouse Family cassette and put it back in its case
- Remove your Lighthouse Family cassette and turn it over (if your cassette player doesn't have auto-reverse)
- Push in the cigarette lighter

- Adjust the passenger door mirror
- Wind down your window
- Pull down your sun visor
- Tune your radio to the Steve Wright show
- To show them your AA badge and flick the Vs

---

 11 STUPID NAMES THE JAPANESE WILL NEVER GIVE THEIR CARS

- The Enola Gay Sedan
- The Oppenheimer 2 litre Estate
- The Jap's Eye 1300 Convertible
- The Death Railway Coupe GLX
- The Pearl Harbor Executive Saloon
- The Nagasaki 1600 DeLuxe
- The Yellow Peril 1500 GTI
- The Dead Dolphin 2 litre Hatchback
- The Kamikaze Supra
- The Hari Kiri 2000 16 Valve
- The Protectionist Trade Policy GL

---

 10 STUPID WAYS TO PASS THE TIME ON THE TRAIN TO WORK

- Try to work out if the girl standing in the corner is wearing culottes or a skirt
- See how long you can hold your breath between stations
- Try to think of alternative headlines for all the advertisements in the carriage. It shouldn't be too difficult
- Have a giggle by reading all the advertisements in the carriage but replacing any word beginning with 'A' by the word 'Twat', and any

word beginning with 'B' by the word 'Bum'.
(e.g. 'British Airways. The world's favourite air-
line' becomes 'Bum Twat. The world's favourite
Twat')
- Try to estimate (to the nearest fifteen minutes)
  how late you're going to be
- Imagine who you'd eat first if the train got
  stuck in a tunnel with the doors jammed, for 72
  hours
- Do the 73 times table in your head (if this
  comes easily, how about recalling all the prime
  numbers between 417 and 1043)
- Pretend to have a convincing twitch
- Try to out-stare the person opposite you until
  they either get up and leave, hit you in the
  head or say something suggestive
- Using your feet, drum through every one of the
  tracks on the latest Prodigy album

---

5 PEOPLE IT'S NOT ADVISABLE TO PICK UP AS HITCHHIKERS

- Anyone who's easily influenced who's seen
  The Hitcher with Rutger Hauer twenty seven
  times
- Anyone carrying a sack of money and a sawn-
  off shot gun
- Anyone wearing a ski mask, especially if it's the
  middle of summer
- Anyone whose best friend was murdered by a
  driver giving them a lift and who's out to get
  revenge
- Anyone who wants to go in completely the
  opposite direction

Once upon a time

7 EGYPTIAN PHARAOHS WHO WERE ALSO PROFESSIONAL BOXERS

- 'Iron Mike' Ramses II
- 'Smokin' Joe' Seti
- 'Battling' Amenophis III
- Ptolemy II 'The Memphis Slugger'
- 'Boom Boom' Horemheb
- 'Sugar Ray' Tuthmosis IV
- King 'KO' Khafre

10 STUPID EGYPTIAN GIFTS TO BRITAIN IN ADDITION TO CLEOPATRA'S NEEDLE

- Cleopatra's bobbin
- Cleopatra's pin cushion
- Cleopatra's cotton reel
- Cleopatra's thimble
- Cleopatra's knitting pattern
- Cleopatra's tape measure
- Cleopatra's Ronco Buttoneer
- Cleopatra's pinking shears
- Cleopatra's crochet hook
- Cleopatra's hem tape

12 UNSCIENTIFIC EXPLANATIONS FOR HOW THOSE HUGE STONES WERE TRANSPORTED FROM WALES TO STONEHENGE

- Suspended beneath a UFO in a teleportation beam
- On the backs of 13,628,359 ants
- On the backs of 5,381,691 stronger ants
- On the back of one veritable Hercules of the ant world
- In the cargo bay of a Lockheed Galaxy
- By magic pixie dust
- Intercity 125 to Swindon, and then by road
- In millions of tiny pieces which were then superglued back together on site
- Carried by ancient Celtic boy scouts during bob-a-job week
- Picked up by giant crows mistaking them for seeds, then dropped when they realised their mistake
- The druids' own version of parcel post
- They were stolen and dumped there

---

8 STUPID PIECES OF FURNITURE IN KING ARTHUR'S CASTLE, IN ADDITION TO HIS ROUND TABLE

- Rectangular Chair
- Square Bookcase
- Octagonal Sideboard
- Diamond-Shaped Cupboard
- Hexagonal Bed
- Elliptical Sofa
- Triangular Bath
- Trapezoid Wardrobe

8 STUPID REASONS WHY THE ROMANS BUILT STRAIGHT ROADS

- To stop the Assyrians opening up corner shops
- The bend had yet to be invented
- Romans had no sense of direction and needed all the help they could get
- They were worried that Celts would smear slippery woad on the corners
- Chariots were not equipped with steering wheels
- They were scared of Druids lurking in dark corners
- If they'd had bends, a legion might not see another legion marching the opposite way and might collide head on
- Romans were notoriously prone to travel sickness

NICKNAMES OF BRITISH PRIME MINISTERS 1855–1924

- Viscount Palmerston ('Baldy')
- Earl Russell ('Dusty')
- The Earl of Derby ('Skipper')
- William Ewart Gladstone ('Basher')
- Benjamin Disraeli, Earl of Beaconsfield ('Spud')
- The Marquis of Salisbury ('Fatty')
- The Earl of Rosebery ('Stinker')
- Arthur James Balfour ('Nobby')
- Sir Henry Campbell-Bannerman ('Pee Wee')
- Herbert Henry Asquith ('Bazza')
- David Lloyd George ('That Welsh Git')
- Andrew Bonar Law ('Randy Andy')
- Stanley Baldwin ('Guffer')
- James Ramsay MacDonald ('Bo-Bo')

14 REASONS TO BE GLAD YOU WEREN'T ALIVE IN THE FOURTEENTH CENTURY

- The Church would burn you alive for having a wart or saying 'Here, kitty, kitty' or being in possession of a broom
- The only cure for a toothache was to smash your head repeatedly against a wall until it hurt worse than your tooth
- You usually died before you were old enough to vote
- But then you didn't have the vote anyway
- People with bubonic plague were everywhere (including your house), and they put you off your dinner
- You had to dance round a fucking maypole every May
- You spent from dawn until dusk up to your knees in shit
- There was no *Loaded* or *FHM* magazine. You had to read the Bible
- But then, you probably couldn't read anyway
- Lepers would come along and breathe on you
- All your orifices officially belonged to the lord of the manor
- By law, you had to practise archery, which is dead boring and really hurts the fingers
- The main source of entertainment was watching a field lie fallow
- You wouldn't be alive now to see Julia Roberts

10 THINGS VIKING BERSERKERS WERE RENOWNED FOR

- Going berserk

- Cutting people's heads off
- Going purple in the face
- Screaming a lot
- Spinning in circles with a two-handed battle axe
- Thrashing about
- Foaming at the mouth
- Glazed expressions
- Dribbling profusely during combat
- Finishing fighting two hours after everybody else

10 THINGS VIKING BERSERKERS WERE NOT RENOWNED FOR

- Baking good cakes
- Well-reasoned debate
- Charm
- Poise
- Elegance
- Cunning battle plans
- Good dress sense
- Having a lot upstairs
- An active sense of irony
- Washing behind their ears

9 STUPID QUIPS MADE BY THE CAPTAIN OF THE TITANIC

- I feel wrecked!
- Ever had that sinking feeling?
- Do you want ice with that?
- Brrrrrr! It's freezing out
- I think I'll crash out for the night

- Bottoms up!
- We'll all go down in history
- Well I'm going to drown my sorrows
- Land ahoy!

COINCIDENCE OR NOT? 8 STUPID DIFFERENCES BETWEEN ABRAHAM LINCOLN AND JOHN F. KENNEDY

- Lincoln had a beard; Kennedy was clean-shaven
- Kennedy was travelling in a car when he was shot; Lincoln was at the theatre
- Lincoln was instrumental in freeing the slaves; Kennedy promised to land an American on the moon and bring him back safely to Earth
- Lincoln was shot by someone called 'John'; Kennedy was shot by someone called 'Lee'
- Lincoln is a town in England; Kennedy is not
- Lincoln was 56 when he died; Kennedy was 46
- Lincoln did not have a space centre named after him; Kennedy did
- Lincoln's first name was 'Abraham'; Kennedy's was 'John'

---

2 STUPID EVENTS IN THE HISTORY OF SEAFARING

- 1412: Prince Henry the Navigator changes his name to 'Prince Henry the Absolutely No Sense Of Direction' in order to inspire more confidence in the crew
- 1474: Bartholomew Diaz discovers the concept of 'North East' and a whole new area of exploration is opened up

Our furry friends

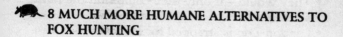

8 MUCH MORE HUMANE ALTERNATIVES TO FOX HUNTING

- Fox stroking
- Fox cuddling
- Fox petting
- Fox tickling
- Fox snuggling
- Fox caressing
- Fox hugging
- Huntsmen hunting

21 POSSIBLE EXPLANATIONS AS TO WHY YOU NEVER SEE GORILLAS WEARING TUXEDOS

- The chimps tease them
- They don't have a credit-card number to leave as security
- They're never invited to any important functions
- They can't afford passage on cruise liners
- There are no gorilla after-dinner speakers
- They prefer casual
- They need bigger pockets to store their bananas
- The orang-utans hired them all first

- They do – it's just hard to see them in all that mist
- Branches of Moss Bros are few and far between in Rwanda
- They feel 'poncy' and won't have their photograph taken
- They can't play snooker to save their lives
- They're over-qualified to get jobs as nightclub bouncers
- They would – if only they could find the right shirt
- London Zoo is strapped for cash
- You're just not in the right place at the right time
- Gorillas wear them only on special occasions. Because the occasion is so special, they also have a shave and are therefore easily mistaken for painters and decorators on their way to a trade gala dinner
- They have nothing to celebrate
- It's been almost thirty years since the Hollywood Premiere of *Planet of the Apes*
- Bright, stripy cycle shorts are considered de-rigueur amongst socially active Silver Backs
- They prefer to eat them

5 VERY SLOW ANIMALS

- A sloth with absolutely no sense of urgency
- A three-legged tortoise
- A snail with time to kill
- A giant panda suffering from severe depression
- A cautious hippo on very thin ice

12 WAYS THAT LASSIE EMBARRASSED HERSELF OFF CAMERA

- Humping Roddy McDowell's leg
- Breaking wind at the precise moment the director yelled, 'Quiet on the Set!'
- Wild alcoholic binges at the Coconut Grove
- Running off with Katherine Hepburn's Oscar and burying it somewhere in the Hollywood Hills
- Worrying Trigger and making Roy Rogers fall off him
- Two-timing Rin Tin Tin with Rex the Wonder Dog
- Sniffing Sam Goldwyn's butt during important production meetings
- Getting into the young Elizabeth Taylor's trailer and urinating over her wardrobe
- Mauling the film critic of the *Los Angeles Times*
- Vociferously campaigning to be cast as Scarlet O'Hara in *Gone With The Wind*
- Scandalous behaviour while out on the town with David Niven and Errol Flynn
- Climbing on to a table in the studio commissary and stealing Victor Mature's sausages

13 ANIMALS THAT ARE NOT OFTEN CONSIDERED AS PETS

- Musk-Ox
- Any other type of Ox
- Black Mambas
- Giant Squids
- Head Lice
- Great One-Horned Rhinoceros

- Soldier Ants
- Black Panthers
- Slugs
- Mastodons (they're extinct, apart from anything else)
- Amoebas
- Dogs with rabies
- Cheese Rolls (they go mouldy after a short while)

---

10 THINGS THE GODFATHER COULD DO WITH THE HORSE'S BODY AFTER PUTTING ITS HEAD IN SOMEONE'S BED

- Sell it to any one of the high-street burger chains
- Have it stuffed and exhibited at an avant-garde gallery as a 'Headless Horse'
- Have it and another one stuffed and exhibited at the same gallery as 'A Pair Of Headless Horses'
- Sew a pig's head on to it and sell it to a freak show as a rare (and dead) example of a pig-horse cross breed
- Take it back to the stud farm and complain it was like this when they got it home and opened the box
- Have a really sick (and extremely messy) intimate relationship with it
- Spread the rumour that it's a hot tip for a big race then make a fortune when loads of people bet on it and it fails to even get out of the stalls
- Put it in a bin liner and leave it outside his house on Tuesday morning
- Scoop out the insides and cut off the front legs,

then hold his nose, get inside the carcass and
go to a fancy-dress party as a centaur
• Use it as a warning for someone with a much
bigger bed

14 ANIMALS WITH STUPID NAMES

• Ocelot
• Aardvark
• Okapi
• Tapir
• Sperm Whale
• Orang-utan
• Bandicoot
• Caribou
• Gecko
• Gnu
• Aye-Aye
• Dingo
• Cuttlefish
• Ring-tailed Lemur

20 REASONS WE SHOULD DECLARE WAR ON THE ANTS

• They're much smaller than us
• They deserve it for getting in the sugar bowl
• They don't have any tanks
• You can have a picnic and fight for your coun-
try at the same time
• A full-scale retaliatory strike will consist of a
bite on the ankle
• You wouldn't have to go further than the back
garden to fight

- When you got sick and tired of the horrors of war you could go back inside your house again
- They're satisfyingly crunchy
- There's little chance of Russian military intervention
- You can declare victory any time you like and no one will be any the wiser
- When you join up, you'll get given weapons with awesome destructive capabilities – like the M16 Magnifying Glass
- It is unlikely that the ants have double agents planted inside military intelligence to betray our secret war plans
- They're even easier to duff over than Iraqis
- It will be good practice for when we declare war on slugs
- They're evil
- Basic training would be short (how much time does it take to learn how to jump up and down?)
- They can't dress up in our uniforms and infiltrate our lines
- They want our women (probably)
- It's them or us (probably)
- We're at war with almost everything else in nature, so why not?

---

 11 ALTERNATIVES TO 'SHOOTING FISH IN A BARREL'

- Harpooning kangaroos in a bathysphere
- Flicking elastic bands at hornets in a jam jar
- Lancing elephants in a box-room
- Nuking Thomson's Gazelles in a bottle bank
- Napalming rhinos in a shed

- Dynamiting monkeys in a box
- Axing sloths in a lift
- Bazooka-ing sheep in a hole
- Poisoning gorillas in a banana silo
- Clubbing baby seals on the tundra
- Making fun of Fergie

---

 12 SANDWICH FILLINGS FOR PEOPLE WHO LIKE THE TASTE OF INSECTS

- Cockroach and cress
- Mosquito and egg salad
- Weevil and tuna
- Flea and coleslaw
- Bluebottle and prawns
- Bumblebee and tomato
- Dung beetle and cheese
- Red ant and salmon pâté
- Dragonfly and Branston pickle
- Earwig and coronation chicken
- Greenfly and lettuce
- Daddy-longlegs and ham on brown bread

---

 10 ANIMALS THAT THE QUICK BROWN FOX JUMPED OVER, APART FROM THE LAZY DOG

- The lethargic hedgehog
- The idle badger
- The slothful tortoise
- The indolent cat
- The workshy fieldmouse
- The languid weasel
- The inert vole
- The sluggish rabbit

- The torpid mole
- The inactive squirrel

---

15 HIT MOVIES WITH ARMADILLOS IN THEM

- Carry On Armadillo (1964)
- Enter The Armadillo (1973)
- Who Framed Roger Armadillo? (1989)
- Three Men And An Armadillo (1991)
- Reservoir Armadillos (1993)
- Indecent Armadillo (1993)
- When Harry Met Armadillo (1989)
- A Clockwork Armadillo (1971)
- Gone With The Armadillo (1939)
- Four Weddings And An Armadillo (1994)
- The Silence Of The Armadillos (1991)
- Seven Brides For Seven Armadillos (1954)
- Armadillo (1976)
- Armadillo II (1978)
- Armadillo III (1981)

 ## 17 THINGS YOUR DOG DOESN'T UNDERSTAND

- That he's not your superior
- The word 'No!'
- Anything else you tell him in plain English
- That the vet isn't an evil fiend bent on killing him
- Why he shouldn't roll in the mud and then take a nap on your bed
- Why you all suddenly leave the room when he has a wind attack
- That you don't find it absolutely hilarious when, late one night, he suddenly starts staring

at an empty corner of the room with teeth
bared and hackles raised
- Precisely what's wrong with practising his
fiercest, gruffest bark at 3 a.m.
- That it's not funny to carry your discarded
underpants into the room with him in front of
guests
- That the furniture is not there for his personal
amusement
- Why it's wrong to back Auntie Joan into a corner and guard her
- Why your leg doesn't enjoy it as much as he
does
- That other dogs' bottoms are not the most fas-
cinating thing in the world
- Why your cat has as much right to sit in the
lounge as he has
- Why he should get into the bathtub if he doesn't
want to
- Why he shouldn't steal the pâté off the table if
he can reach it
- Why he shouldn't do exactly what he wants,
basically

 **10 AMAZING BOOKS BY THOMAS HARDY
ABOUT FISH**

- The Bream of Casterbridge
- Tess of the Herring
- Far From the Madding Shoal
- Jude the Halibut
- The Brisket Major
- Desperate Tench
- Life's Little Minnows
- The Fins of Ethel Sardine

- Under the Grey-Green Sea
- The Return of the Salmon

...AND 10 MORE BY CHARLES DICKENS

- A Tale of Two Trout
- Haddock and Son
- A Christmas Fish
- Oliver Tiddler
- Nicholas Coelacanth
- David Codderfield
- The Whitebait Papers
- The Old Curiosity Mackerel
- Little Coley
- Edwin Skate

---

11 CREATURES WHICH SOUND QUITE RUDE

- The bustard
- The great tit
- The poodle
- The horny toad
- The cockatoo
- The pronghorn antelope
- The winkle
- The cockle
- The cock
- The ass
- The sperm whale

RIN TIN TIN'S 6 MOST MEMORABLE LINES

- Bow-wow
- Wuff!
- Whine!
- Ruff-ruff-ruff!
- Aowwwwwwwww!
- Grrr! Arf! Arf!

 ## 11 WAYS IN WHICH HEDGEHOGS CAN BE USED TO ENRICH OUR EVERYDAY LIVES

- As deliciously wriggly back scratchers
- As a viable alternative to hamsters for masochistic perverts
- Scraped across freshly iced cakes to give pleasing patterns
- Hairbrushes with their own charming personalities
- Reassuring 'guard dogs' for those who are intensely phobic about worms
- Emergency acupuncture appliances
- If fox hunting is banned, bored members of the gentry could train packs of hedgehogs to hunt garden grubs which may threaten farm livestock
- Put one on your face and pretend to be Rory McGrath (if you're really at a loose end)
- Man and nature in harmony for Artexing
- A time-saving device for a professional balloon burster
- As a police roadblock to joyriders with a conscience

14 THINGS THE DINOSAURS DIDN'T DO WHEN THEY RULED THE EARTH

- Cover their spikes and horny plates with robes of ermine and mink
- Give a Christmas message to all the other dinosaurs
- Receive £40 million a year, virtually tax free
- Inspire smaller dinosaurs to say 'That Brontosaurus, he does a bloody good job. I wouldn't have his job...'
- Go on walkabouts and not eat anyone smaller than they were
- Get married at Westminster Abbey
- Go to a charity premiere of *When Dinosaurs Ruled The Earth*
- Visit other land masses on state visits
- Award honours to other dinosaurs who have shown the greatest contribution to evolution
- Have children that went skiing half the year (the ice age had yet to occur)
- Open the dinosaur parliament (AKA 'The House Of Lords')
- Keep ancient ancestors of the corgi as pets
- Appear on stamps and coinage
- Ride about in a prehistoric coach, waving inanely

Playtime

16 STUPID THINGS YOU'RE GUARANTEED TO FIND AT A BRITISH SEASIDE RESORT

- A beach littered with rusty tin cans, oil, bottles, dog turds, ice-lolly sticks and a dead seagull
- A decrepid 'Esplanade Cafe' that's always shut
- Groups of lager louts sitting on the pier railings holding pint glasses and mooning at passing families
- Waving, cooing pensioners with thick coats and expressions smiling inanely from the promenade train
- Unpredictable weather (although most days are cold, damp and miserable)
- No hot water in your B & B after 3.00 p.m. (and precious little before that), a list of restrictions about ninety feet long and a landlady resembling Demis Roussos who'll knock on your door every hour without fail to make sure that you haven't brought any women back to your room
- The sea maintained at a constant 4°C with raw sewage being regularly piped in to create that familiar grey-brown 'Christ, I'm not going in there!' look
- Prats with metal detectors pacing up and down the beach like expectant fathers
- Fat, ugly people changing their swimming costumes behind far too skimpy towels
- Loudspeakers on the promenade that constantly

blast out a distorted Chris Evans
- Wankers on roller skates and skateboards
- Stray dogs 'doing it' behind dilapidated beach huts
- Boring illuminations with one bulb in three that doesn't work
- Cannon and Ball (supported by The Spinners) perpetually topping the bill at the Palace Winter Gardens
- Hordes of stupid Spanish-looking students
- Discos that still play Frankie Goes To Hollywood and Earth, Wind and Fire, and which are filled with guys wearing white socks and sovereign rings who are on the pull – getting nowhere and settling for pushing each other through plate glass windows on the esplanade at 2.00 a.m.

 ## 14 THINGS TO DO WHILE WAITING IN THE QUEUE IN THE POST OFFICE

- Go through the menopause
- Read *War and Peace*
- Read *War and Peace* in the original Russian, after mastering the language
- Pitch camp between the leaflets for orthopaedic beds and the Truprint envelopes
- Raise a family
- Think about those lucky bastards who are on the NHS waiting list instead
- Expire of old age
- Wish you were in jail (where at least there's a chance of parole...)
- Decide that nothing is worth this waiting, let alone four frigging first-class stamps and a

Mercury phonecard
- Become a great-grandparent
- Decide it would be quicker to deliver the letter to Inverness on foot
- Pray the post office doesn't get closed down before you get to the counter
- Do yourself actual physical injury after being forced to watch the same life-assurance ad on the post-office video screen for the 82nd time
- Count how many times a counter closes just before you reach it

---

 11 OTHER SHAPES FOOTBALLS COULD BE (BUT AREN'T FOR VERY GOOD REASONS)

- Rectangular
- Sort of blobby with one end sticking up
- Sort of blobby with the other end sticking up
- Cubed
- Pyramid-shaped
- Mini Metro-shaped
- Sort of round, but with a star and a twisty bit in the middle
- Pancake-shaped
- Trapezoid
- A shape that exists in six dimensions simultaneously and can only be expressed as a mathematical equation
- Rugby-ball-shaped – because then they would be rugby balls

13 STUPID NAMES TO CALL YOUR NEW RESTAURANT

- Vommo's
- El Botulissimo
- Scabby Joe's
- The Chukka Tandoori
- Monsieur Rip-off's
- Il Trattoria de Puke
- Dahmer's of Covent Garden
- The Mad Cow
- Septics of Mayfair
- Le Toilet
- Istanbul's Finest
- The Filthy Kitchen
- Dennis Nilsen's

 ## 10 SPORTS STARS NOT CALLED STEVE

- Tim Henman
- Jonah Alomo
- Paul 'Gazza' Gascoigne
- Prince Naseem Hamed
- Tiger Woods
- Hulk Hogan
- Ruud Gullit
- Michael Jordan
- Ian Wright
- Rory Underwood

 ## 10 STUPID THINGS TO DO WITH A TELEPHONE IN YOUR SPARE TIME

- Make obscene phone calls from your office to

your home answerphone
- Ring up the Tasmanian speaking clock, leave the receiver off the hook and go out for a leisurely walk
- Marry it
- Make obscene phone calls to the cricket score line
- Use it often (if you aren't a multi-millionaire)
- Ring up people you don't know and ask for Barry
- Ring up people you do know and ask for Barry
- Ring up Directory Enquiries and ask for ten numbers you already know
- Ring up the AA or RAC and pretend to be in distress in the remotest part of the Lake District
- Ring up any 0898 number

 ## 13 STUPID PITCHES FOR MOVIES

- 'It's *Mission Impossible* meets *The Teletubbies*...'
- 'It's *Jaws* meets *Prêt à Porter* in space...'
- 'It's *Three Weddings and a Funeral* meets *Mortal Kombat*...'
- 'It's *Mr Bean* meets *The Exorcist*...'
- 'It's Charlie Chaplin meets *Aliens*...'
- 'It's *The Lion King* meets *The Godfather* meets *Titanic*...in space...'
- 'It's *Lawrence of Arabia* meets four different kinds of cheeses...'
- 'It's *Planet of the Apes* meets *Planet of the Apes*...'
- 'It's *The Muppets* meets *Deep Throat*...'
- 'It's whatever's in your pocket meets *The Terminator*...'
- 'It's "Mandy" by Barry Manilow played non-stop over pictures of decaying fruit for 95 minutes'

- 'It's *Xanadu* meets *Heaven's Gate* meets *Don't Stop The Music* meets *Shanghai Express* meets *Ishtar*...'
- 'It's Chuck Norris meets *Digby the Biggest Dog In The World*...'

 10 STUPID PEOPLE YOU DON'T WANT SITTING NEAR YOU IN THE CINEMA

- Anyone with glazed eyes who makes little gasping sounds under his breath at all the gory moments in the film
- Someone who is obviously accompanying a blind friend, because he has to explain what's going on every single moment of the film...
- Someone who eats their popcorn like an asthmatic pig
- Someone who has seen the film before and insists on telling his friend 'This is a really good bit...' or 'Don't look!', every two minutes
- A child who has just had the largest-sized tub of sugared popcorn and four Westlers and is looking around for somewhere to be sick
- An old man who is fast asleep and snoring
- The local lads' contingent, who act like they're still on the building site whenever any character takes an item of clothing off (even if it's a hat)
- Someone who thinks the back of your chair (and your collar) is his footrest
- Someone who has dropped a Callard & Bowser down by her feet and is determined to root around and find it, even if it takes her the whole film...
- Someone in a grubby raincoat who you suspect might be frantically rubbing himself under cover of darkness

14 THINGS YOU SHOULDN'T DO IN A PUBLIC LIBRARY

- Hold a shouting contest
- Hold a barbecue, using volumes of the Encyclopaedia Britannica as briquettes
- Do your impression of *Krakatoa – East of Java*
- Fly a remote-controlled aircraft
- Pop a succession of crisp packets
- Busk
- Hold an impromptu demonstration of primal scream therapy
- Ask for particular books through a megaphone
- Piss off the librarian by asking for *Fly Fishing* by J. R. Hartley
- Demonstrate your yodelling prowess
- Dress up as a leading Nazi and burn anything that looks fairly intelligent
- Hold a commendably ethnic display of Greek plate smashing
- Put a sheet over your head, and make ghost noises behind the occult section
- Snigger and point at the people looking at books on how to cope with VD

6 STUPID THINGS THAT ALWAYS HAPPEN DURING A GAME OF MONOPOLY

- A fight over who gets to be the car, the iron or the dog (as if it really matters)
- No one understanding how the mortgages work
- Arguments over the rules of 'Free Parking'
- Someone saying something predictable when the card with 'You have won second prize in a beauty contest' is picked up

- Someone saying, 'Wouldn't it be great if all this money was real!'
- Everyone gets bored halfway through

 10 STUPID GAMES OR SPORTS TO PLAY ON YOUR OWN

- Kiss Chase
- American Football
- Tug of War
- Spin The Bottle
- Pictionary
- Pass The Parcel
- Hide and Seek
- Postman's Knock
- Cricket
- 4 x 100 metres relay

 12 STUPID NAMES TO CALL YOUR RACEHORSE

- Lame Boy
- A Little Slow
- Lose Your Shirt
- Dunracing Lad
- Last Past The Post
- Steward's Enquiry
- Doped-Up Git
- Cat-Meat Certainty
- Limpy Sam
- Rank Outsider
- Knacker's Choice
- Asthmatic Lass

10 STUPID THINGS TO USE AS THE BATON IN A RELAY RACE

- A small cactus
- A scorpion
- Anything covered in superglue
- Anything white hot
- Anything securely manacled to your wrist
- A lit stick of dynamite
- An anvil
- A baton-shaped piece of margarine
- Your willie
- Someone else's willie

 10 STUPID CLUBS AND SOCIETIES TO JOIN

- The Plastic Bag Appreciation Society
- The Royal Society for Putting Things Back in the Wrong Place
- The League of People with Nothing Better to Do
- The Vole Fanciers' Self-help Group
- The Unipeds' Marquetry and Standing Upright Club
- The Guild of Nose Bleed Sufferers
- The Society for the Prevention of Something We've Forgotten
- The Bobby Davro Fan Club
- Friends of the Bourbon Biscuit
- Teetotallers Anonymous

10 STUPID THINGS TO DO IF YOU COLLECT STAMPS

- Cut the perforations off because they look untidy
- Staple them into your album
- Only collect stamps from countries beginning with 'Y'
- After you've catalogued and cross-indexed them, feed them into a paper shredder
- Stick your most valuable ones on an envelope and post them to a fictitious address in New Zealand
- Go into Stanley Gibbons and ask to see the monkeys
- Colour them all in felt pen and pretend they're Penny Blacks
- File them in order based on the third letter of the country's name
- Draw glasses and a moustache on the Queen's portrait
- Collect coins by mistake

15 STUPID THINGS TO DO IN THE SUPERMARKET

- Fill a trolley completely to the top, get to the checkout and wait for the cashier to total it all up before saying, 'Oh...sorry...I've only got 20p on me – so you'll just have to put it all back now, won't you?'...And walk out
- When other shoppers aren't looking, throw lots of useless or highly expensive products into their trolley, to cause confusion, delays and even possibly kicking and biting fights at

the checkout

- Put itching powder all over the baby seat of a trolley so that the next kiddie who sits there totally freaks out and embarrasses his mother
- Pretend to have an epileptic fit and thrash your way down the aisles, knocking tins and bottles in every direction
- Before you pay for anything, rip off all the prices and scribble over the bar codes, so that someone has to go and check on every single price
- Pretend to be Arabic. Haggle at the till during a busy Friday night, screaming things like, 'By the Beard of The Prophet, I shall not give you more than 35p for this cake mix!'
- Pretend to be Arabic and shove groceries down your gown
- Get together with some friends and have Ben Hur-type trolley races round and round the frozen foods counter
- Unwrap a Mars Bar and stick it up your bottom. Storm into the supermarket at the busiest time imaginable and scream, 'This Mars Bar's got pooh all over it and I bought it from this store!'
- Tell all the young children you see that the sweets next to the cash register are free and they can help themselves
- Sellotape half a cucumber to your forehead and charge about, pretending to be a rhinoceros and making snorty noises until you are finally thrown out
- Run around the store, stamping your feet violently and yelling, 'I got another cockroach!'
- Fill your trolley until it's overflowing, go to the checkout and tell the cashier that, before you spend a single solitary penny, you want written

assurance that not one single ingredient of any product originates in Serbia, Chile, El Salvador or New Zealand

- Put on a white coat and pretend you're an assistant. When a customer asks where they can find something, tell them to mind their own business...
- Put on a white coat and pretend you're an assistant. Offer to take someone's trolley out to their car. Wheel their trolley straight into the middle of the road and violently tip it over...

 ## 10 STUPID THINGS THAT TASTE MARGINALLY BETTER THAN BEAUJOLAIS NOUVEAU

- Sump drainings after a 20,000-mile oil change
- The contents of a catheter bag
- Dog spittle
- Rancid semolina
- Fifteen-year-old vinegar
- Cough medicine
- Shampoo
- Processed sewage
- Raw sewage
- Guinness

 ## 10 STUPID THINGS YOU'LL NEVER SEE AT A BOWLS MATCH

- The crowd on their feet
- The home supporters singing ''Ere we go, 'ere we go, 'ere we go!'
- The away supporters singing 'Who's that wanker in the white!'

- A tackle above the knee
- A streaker who's under 55
- Much sign of human life
- The referee award an indirect free kick
- The crowd protesting about a handball
- A nice turn of speed
- An 'off the ball' incident

---

 11 MORE INTERESTING THINGS TO DO THAN WATCH A GAME OF CRICKET

- Count the number of cars you see on a 110 mile motorway drive
- Paint a ceiling in undercoat
- Pluck every one of the hairs on your arms with tweezers
- Watch a game of bowls
- Play solitaire 78 consecutive times
- Rewire all the plugs in your house
- Catalogue all the food in your house according to weight, brand name in alphabetical order and colour of packaging
- Read everything by Proust
- Visit a garden centre
- Go to night school to learn tax accounting
- Ring up a financial advisor and ask for advice

 ELLE ('THE BODY') MACPHERSON'S 9 FAVOURITE CHESS MOVES

- P–R3
- Q–KKt2
- P–K4
- R–K1

- QR–K1
- K–K2
- P–QKt4
- R–B3
- B–KB4

 THE 66 MOST STUPID GAMES AVAILABLE FOR THE SONY PLAYSTATION

- Scrumping
- Cross-Dresser!
- Angina!
- Dental Decay
- You Are Robin Cook's Secretary
- The Severn Valley Water Authority
- Arable Farmer!
- Spitting Contest
- Virgin!
- C of E Youth Club Pentathalon
- Emergency Sewer Drainage
- Night Emissions!
- Catatonia!
- Acne Breakout!
- Mind Your Foreskin
- Mini Clubman
- Stroke My Thighs Vicar
- Post Mortem
- Sore Throat
- Geography Multiple Choice
- GCSE's (Just Like The Real Thing!)
- Polish Scrabble
- Cold Sore
- Lumbago!!
- Liquorice Allsorts
- You Are Frank Ifield

- Congenital Illness
- Salvation Army Church Parade
- Andi Peter's Strip Poker Game
- Join The Dots
- Match Wits With Henry Kelly
- Willie Warfare!
- Egg and Spoon Race
- You Are e e cummings!
- Unrequited Love
- Split Ends!
- Dead Puppy
- VDU Screen Radiation
- Feed The Ducks
- Dostoyevsky – The Adventure Continues!
- Whoops – There Goes Lunch!
- Mollusc
- Anchovies with Everything!
- Play Chess with Elaine Paige
- Gordon Brown's Laugh A Minute Game
- Ceasefire!
- Season Ticket
- Phlegm Attack! (2 discs)
- Bomb Benny Green
- Incontinence Deluge
- H-Block Dirty Protest
- Genital Mishaps!
- You Have Elvis's Brain
- Kangaroo Vet
- Mini-Cab Driver
- Emergency Plumber
- Pro-Am Quoits
- Lara Croft – Seamstress!
- Virtual Hopscotch!
- Spring Cleaning 3000AD
- 3D Bakewell Tarts
- Algebra Apocalypse!

- CyberOtters!
- Sim Gardening
- Ultimate Toaster!
- Interactive Solitaire

---

 14 STUPID PLACES TO GO ON HOLIDAY

- Beirut
- Where you work
- Your next-door neighbours' house
- Birmingham
- The place you went last year and hated
- Kennels
- The local video shop
- Into the cupboard under the stairs
- Chernobyl
- Anywhere down wind of Chernobyl
- Libya
- Anywhere else beginning with 'L' (including Lesotho, Liechtenstein and Laos)
- Directly in the path of Hurricane Sharon
- Majorca

---

 10 TOP SOCCER PLAYERS' FAVOURITE ISLANDS

- Danny Blanchflower [Madagascar]
- David Beckham [Sumatra]
- Paul 'Gazza' Gascoigne [Switzerland]
- Bobby Charlton [Tasmania]
- Sir Stanley Matthews [Cuba]
- Andy Cole [the Isle of Wight]
- Tony Adams [Kos]
- Les Ferdinand [Baffin Island]
- Kenny Dalglish [Tobago]

- Steve McManaman [Corsica]

 9 STUPID THINGS YOUR HOLIDAY BROCHURE SAYS (AND WHAT THEY REALLY MEAN)

- Well-established resort... (This resort used to be quite nice...until the British discovered it. Now it's a cross between Hades, Saturday night in Ilford and a bucket of pooh)
- ...Becomes busy between May and September.. (Most of the town is unsafe between May and September, unless you support Millwall)
- ...A popular destination for the young and with-it... (Great if you like arseholes, otherwise avoid like the plague)
- ...A very popular, traditional, budget-priced hotel... (This two-star hotel is utter shite, but we get very preferential terms for using it. Staff are indifferent, hygiene is Turkish in its awfulness and, if you stand outside the main entrance, some drunken British thug will invariably piss off the balcony on to your head)
- ...Cosmopolitan clientele... (no chance whatsoever of getting a sunbed, because the place is full of Germans)
- ...Convenient location... (Miles from the beach, but with the overpowering smell of untreated sewage, cheap suntan lotion and BO wafting off it, that's a blessing as far as we are concerned)
- ...Now under new management... (The old manager is still in a coma, following last year's 'Welcome British Holidaymakers' Sangria party which got tragically out of hand)
- ...British food served... (Juan the chef has been

warned that, unless he wants his fingers broken for a third time, there's going to be no more foreign muck served up)

- ...Always plenty to do... (Drinking, fighting the Krauts and Dagos, more drinking, building obscene sandcastles on the beach, more bevvies, some things that will make *News at Ten* back home, dodging the Spanish National Guard, more bevvies, vomit in town square, vomit in 'The Londoner' Disco, vomit off the balcony, get food poisoning and have to spend the rest of the holiday in bed)

 10 STUPID OCCUPATIONS TO PUT ON YOUR PASSPORT

- Ocelot masturbator
- Criminal mastermind
- Drugs baron
- Professional sperm donor
- Locomotive juggler
- Self-employed wiggly dancer
- Catheter fitter to the crowned heads of Europe
- Napalm taster
- Unicellular life form
- Civil servant

What a **wonderful** world

 8 RIVALS TO THE INFAMOUS 'BERMUDA TRIANGLE'

- The Bahamas Oblong
- The Monserrat Trapezium
- The St Lucia Circle
- The Jamaican Ellipse
- The Barbados Rhomboid
- The Trinidad and Tobago Parallelogram
- The Antigua Hexagon
- The Kennington Oval

 6 STUPID AIRCRAFT IN TODAY'S ROYAL SWAZILAND AIRFORCE

- 1 x ex-Pan American Airlines Ford TriMotor
- 1 x Bleriot XI Monoplane replica
- 4 x Hot Air balloons with aggressive faces painted on the wicker baskets
- 2 x Sopwith Camels
- $\frac{1}{2}$x ex-Spanish airforce Messerschmitt Me109E (used for spares)

- 1 x Glossy 10 x 8 inch colour photo of an F-15, pinned to the control tower noticeboard

---

5 COUNTRIES WITH FLAGS THAT ARE QUITE DIFFICULT TO DRAW

- Bhutan. (Rectangle divided into red and orange triangles with some kind of ornate Chinese-looking serpent in the middle)
- Dominica. (Something that looks like a green parrot in a red circle, surrounded by ten green stars. The circle is in the centre of a yellow, black and white striped cross with green bits in the corners)
- South Korea. (A ball made up of interlocking 'squiggly' red and blue shapes on a white background. Around the ball are four different patterns that look as though they're from a 'Spot The Odd One Out' test)
- Papua, New Guinea. (Rectangle divided into two triangles. The black one contains six white stars, four big ones and two smaller ones, while the red triangle contains some sort of tropical bird with a long tail)
- Brazil. (Yellow diamond shape set in a green rectangle. In the yellow diamond is a sort of blue globe with a band running where the equator should be. There's some writing or symbols in this band but the picture in the reference book we're using is too small to make it out properly)

11 STUPID THINGS TO TELL FOREIGN TOURISTS IN LONDON

- It's considered good luck to stroke a guardsman's busby
- The nearest tube station to Buckingham Palace is Ongar
- You can fish for salmon off Westminster Bridge
- Horatio Nelson was the founder of London and had four pet lions
- It is almost obligatory to haggle with taxi drivers over the fare
- The traditional term of address for a London policeman is, 'wanker'
- A yellow line indicates free parking for one hour (a double yellow line indicates two hours)
- There is no speed limit along the Embankment between 11.00 p.m. and 5.00 a.m.
- All Commonwealth citizens are entitled to one private audience with the Queen each year. Simply present yourself at the main gate of Buckingham Palace in formal dress
- The Old Kent Road is famed for its gay pubs
- In summer, nude sunbathing is permitted only in one of the Royal Parks; this is St James' Park, off The Mall

 91 PLACES IN AMERICA WHICH, ALTHOUGH REAL, SOUND STUPID

- Arab, Alabama
- Avon, Alabama
- Bibb, Alabama
- Coy, Alabama
- Lower Peach Tree, Alabama

- Moody, Alabama
- Opp, Alabama
- Pisgah, Alabama
- Prattville, Alabama
- Snead, Alabama
- Wetumpka, Alabama
- King Salmon, Alaska
- Bagdad, Arizona
- Chloride, Arizona
- El Mirage, Arizona
- Tuba City, Arizona
- Winkelman, Arizona
- Biggers, Arkansas
- Flippin, Arkansas
- Grubbs, Arkansas
- Tontitown, Arkansas
- Weiner, Arkansas
- Loleta, California
- Lompoc, California
- Pismo Beach, California
- Truckee, California
- Weimar, California
- Dinosaur, Colorado
- Hygiene, Colorado
- Security, Colorado
- Swink, Colorado
- Orange, Connecticut
- The Norman G. Wilder Wildlife Area, Delaware
- Cocoa, Florida
- Homosassa, Florida
- Ponce De Leon, Florida
- Bibb City, Georgia
- Chickamunga, Georgia
- Experiment, Georgia
- Montezuma, Georgia
- Social Circle, Georgia

- Zebulon, Georgia
- Fruitland, Idaho
- Idaho, Idaho
- Energy, Illinois
- Kankakee, Illinois
- Odin, Illinois
- Vermillion, illinois
- Munster, Indiana
- Poseyville, Indiana
- Santa Claus, Indiana
- Tippecanoe, Indiana
- Early, Iowa
- Lost Nation, Iowa
- Mechanicsville, Iowa
- Titonka, Iowa
- Pratt, Iowa
- Tonganoxie, Iowa
- Big Clifty, Kentucky
- Cranks, Kentucky
- Flat Lick, Kentucky
- Raccoon, Kentucky
- Zebulon, Kentucky
- Grosse Tete, Louisiana
- West Peru, Maine
- Princess Anne, Maryland
- Whiskey Bottom, Maryland
- Dorothy Pond, Massachusetts
- North Uxbridge, Massachusetts
- West Acton, Massachusetts
- Ovid, Michigan
- Vulcan, Michigan
- Knob Noster, Missouri
- Pilot Knob, Missouri
- Flathead, Montana
- Cheesequake, New Jersey
- Truth or Consequences, New Mexico

- Dickey, North Dakota
- Gackle, North Dakota
- Dry Run, Ohio
- Mingo Junction, Ohio
- Cement, Oklahoma
- Talent, Oregon
- Berks, Pennsylvania
- Wounded Knee, South Dakota
- Soddy-Daisy, Tennessee
- Deaf Smith, Texas
- Lolita, Texas
- Bland, Virginia
- Isle of Wight, Virginia
- Belgium, Wisconsin

THE 2 THINGS THAT ARE FUNDAMENTALLY WRONG WITH BELGIUM AS A NATION

- It exists
- Belgians live there

---

10 UNSUITABLE NAMES FOR BRUTAL FASCIST DICTATORS

- Fred
- Chuck
- Elvis
- Franky
- Bert
- Bobby
- Benny
- Nobby
- Tim
- Ian

✈ 36 *REAL* PLACES IN AMERICA WHICH SOUND RUDE

- Boggstown, Indiana
- Hornell, New York
- Beaver, Kentucky
- Trussville, Alabama
- Prattville, Alabama
- Fruitdale, Alabama
- Bald Knob, Arkansas
- Bent, Colorado
- Grays Knob, Kentucky
- French Lick, Indiana
- Floyds Knob, Indiana
- Lolita, Texas
- Rogersville, Kentucky
- Flushing, Ohio
- Sodus, New York
- Cockeysville, Maryland
- Colon, Michigan
- Big Beaver, Pennsylvania
- Climax, Michigan
- Licking, Missouri
- Big Horn, Wyoming
- Pollock, Idaho
- Coxsackie, New York
- The Little Big Horn, Montana
- Butte Valley, Nevada
- Hooker, Nebraska
- Biggers, Missouri
- Cokato, Minnesota
- Butte City, California
- Crested Butte, Colorado
- Willimantic, Connecticut
- Tampa, Florida
- Peoria, Illinois

- Effingham, Illinois
- Intercourse, Pennsylvania
- Wanker's Corner, Oregon

 ## THE TOP 10 CAUSES OF DEATH IN BELGIUM

- Boredom
- Falling off bicycles
- The stress of playing Belgian Trivial Pursuit
- Shock induced by something interesting suddenly happening
- Suicide after being refused an emigration permit
- Accidental exposure to a fairly interesting paperback or magazine
- Falling into a coma and having Belgian doctors try to revive you by playing you a personal message from Belgian's top pop star
- Overdosing on chocolate truffles
- Exhaustion brought about by trying to find something interesting to do on Saturday night
- Simply losing the will to live

 ## 7 THINGS THE JAPANESE KILL WHICH THEY SHOULDN'T

- Whales
- Dolphins
- Porpoises
- Anything else that is endangered
- The Western Electronics Industry
- Any concept of fair trading practices
- POWs

11 THINGS IT MUST BE VERY EASY TO SELL TO THE JAPANESE

- Elevator shoes
- Plastic yellow dick extensions
- Penis enlargers
- Dental braces
- Harpoons
- Blue whale ashtrays
- Anything that was once an integral part of an endangered species
- A self-help book entitled How To Work Harder and Die Younger
- A matching set of dolphin-skin luggage
- Anything their company says they should have
- The idea that they can totally ignore what the rest of the world thinks

---

11 THINGS THAT THE BELGIANS ARE NOT VERY GOOD AT

- Throwing wild parties
- Letting their hair down
- Pop music
- Holding their drink
- Telling dirty jokes
- Starting trends
- Vandalism
- Football hooliganism
- Revolutionising the way we live
- Making major motion pictures
- Celebrating (but, to be fair, they have never had anything to celebrate)

11 THINGS THAT THE BELGIANS ARE GOOD AT

- Staying at home with a good book
- Listening to the wireless
- Keeping the garden and allotment in good order
- Making luxurious confectionery
- Knitting and fretwork
- Wearing sensible sweaters and comfortable shoes
- Knowing when they need a haircut
- Remembering people's birthdays
- Keeping neat scrapbooks of recipes and do-it-yourself tips
- Washing their cars at the weekend
- Masturbating

---

 8 UNOFFICIAL BLACK MARKET CURRENCIES OF TURKEY

- Bribes
- Black market US dollars
- Pretty young boys
- Opiates
- Squat-thrusts
- Lambs sold into wool slavery
- Second-hand copies of All-Naked Bashi Bazouks
- Reach-arounds

12 THINGS WHICH LOUIS ARMSTRONG SHOULD HAVE MENTIONED IN 'WHAT A WONDERFUL WORLD' – BUT DIDN'T

- Oral sex
- Diet Cola
- Powerful but gentle laxatives
- Porn on the internet
- Anti-premature-ejaculation creams
- Taramasalata
- Cadbury's
- Disneyland
- Easy credit
- Contraceptive devices
- Bank holidays
- Flushing toilets and toilet paper

---

15 THINGS WHICH LOUIS ARMSTRONG WOULDN'T HAVE EVEN CONSIDERED MENTIONING IN 'WHAT A WONDERFUL WORLD'

- Sudden death
- Hospital anaesthetists who get the gases mixed up and leave you with the IQ of a stick of parsley
- Martin Bormann
- Tonsilitis
- Old dogs with a chronic flatulence problem
- BO
- Difficult sums
- Scabby bits of your body
- The East European motor industry
- Income tax
- Commuting

- Perverts with your phone number
- Phone bills
- The Japanese
- Pot noodles

5 STUPID PLACES TO GO ON HOLIDAY IF YOU WANT A SERIOUS SUN TAN

- The Falkland Islands
- Alaska
- Greenland
- The South Pole
- Manchester

11 PLACES IN GREAT BRITAIN NAMED AFTER CREATURES

- Catford
- Isle of Dogs
- Wolverhampton
- Lizard
- Cowley
- Oxford
- Leighton Buzzard
- Swanage
- Cowes
- Wales
- Shrewsbury

Back to school

5 PUNISHMENTS MORE PAINFUL THAN SIX OF THE BEST

- Seven of the best
- A baker's dozen of the best
- 83,000 of the best
- Six and a half of the best
- Having your hands chopped off in the school stationery guillotine

10 STUPID WAYS TO CHEAT AT EXAMS

- Use an ex-WWII U-boat periscope to see the answers of the candidate sitting directly in front of you
- Take all your textbooks into the exam hall, hidden up your jumper
- Communicate with a friend outside the exam hall by means of a mobile phone
- Write the answers in reverse on your tongue in waterproof ink. When you need to see them, stick your tongue out and look in a hand mirror
- Find out who's setting the paper and employ a team of private detectives to follow them around for a while until they dig up some dirt. Then threaten blackmail unless you're supplied

with the answers

- Make all your textbooks invisible so you can carry them into the exam hall without arousing suspicion
- Have your course notes tattooed all down your legs. When you need to check an answer, just remove your trousers or stockings...
- Develop your latent psychic powers until you're able to read the mind of the class swot sitting twelve desks away
- Travel forwards in time and talk to yourself coming out of the exam hall to find out what the questions were
- Put down the first answer that comes into your head, then change reality to match your answers

---

 ## 13 STUPID WORDS OR PHRASES YOU USUALLY FIND IN YOUR SCHOOL REPORT

- Tries hard
- Lazy
- Easily distracted
- Could do better
- Very disruptive
- Must concentrate
- Bad influence
- Heart not in it
- Inattentive
- Steady progress
- Average
- Sadly lacking
- Class comedian

11 STUPID THINGS YOU'LL ALWAYS FIND AT THE VERY BOTTOM OF YOUR CHILD'S SCHOOL BAG

- Someone else's gym shorts
- A leaky biro
- A boiled sweet with fluff stuck all over it
- One smelly plimsoll
- Sandwich crusts
- Something black, sticky and totally unidentifiable
- A crumpled-up school form you were meant to have received four months ago
- A gaudy pocket calculator with the batteries missing
- A broken ruler covered in doodles
- The school tie that went missing last term
- A joke plastic spider

 10 WORDS YOU DON'T WANT TO SEE ON YOUR CHILD'S REPORT CARD

- Klepto
- Cretin
- Dense
- Incapable
- Worst
- Bully
- Chain smoker
- Failure
- Despised
- Tasty

7 STUPID THINGS TO TELL YOUR CHILDREN ON THEIR FIRST DAY AT SCHOOL

- Teachers should always be referred to as 'Mrs Nobface'
- Bad ghosts live in the school toilets
- If you don't like it, just raise your hand and they'll let you go home
- Spitting at other children will help you make lots of new friends
- I'll come and collect you after an hour
- If you need to go to the toilet, let the teacher know by dropping your trousers
- Lessons don't start until 11 a.m., so there's no hurry to get there, is there?

 11 STUPID THINGS THEY TEACH YOU IN MATHS THAT MEAN BUGGER ALL WHEN YOU LEAVE SCHOOL

- Logarithms
- Matrices
- Vectors
- Quadrilatic equations
- Long division
- Topography
- Working out the lowest common denominator
- Binary arithmetic
- Slide rules
- Algebra
- How long it would take three men to dig seven holes at twice the speed

Mind and body

 14 STUPID EXCUSES TO GIVE AT THE
CASUALTY WARD WHEN YOU'VE GOT A BEER
BOTTLE STUCK UP YOU

- It was on the chair and I sat on it without any clothes on
- Aliens put it there. They ran out of rectal implants but it was lucky they had a crate of Labatts
- I lost my bottle opener and was trying to get the top off with my sphincter of steel
- I misread the label
- It must have got caught up in my Y-fronts in the washing machine
- I was just showing my flatmate what happened in *ER* last week
- I was just showing my flatmate what happened in *Stars In Their Eyes* last week
- It's to do with a religious festival. You infidel dogs would not understand
- I accidentally swallowed a magnet last week and it unfortunately attracted the beer-bottle cap
- I ran out of cucumbers
- My friend and I were playing catch in the nude and I bent over at the wrong time
- It's a bottle of Kaliber; it's the best thing you can do with it

- I keep my suppositories in the same place as I keep my beer and it was dark
- The hamster was thirsty...

15 STUPID THINGS TO SAY WHEN VISITING A SICK RELATIVE

- So, how long have you got then?
- Need any help with the rectal thermometer?
- Breathe on me! Breathe on me!
- God, you look like shit!
- Can I have first dibs on your jewellery?
- Mrs Higgins down the road had that. One day, fit as a fiddle. The next...
- You'll never guess who I saw hanging about outside your ward – the Grim Reaper
- Phworrr! You smell. I'm going to have to leave now
- I thought only sheep caught that...
- Fire! Fire! Everybody out! Quickly!
- The will's in the cupboard under the stairs, isn't it?
- Strewth! You look forty years older. No wonder I didn't recognise you!
- It starts as a cold, yes...
- You're hallucinating: I'm not really here
- So, just two weeks, eh? What, oh, they hadn't told you...

11 STUPID PLACES TO PUT YOUR FINGERS

- Around Jean-Claude Van Damme's throat
- Down Jean-Claude Van Damme's boxer shorts
- Within six inches of a pit bull terrier

- In your eyes, while you're driving at 70 mph
- In your ears, when you're waiting for a crucial phone call
- In an electric socket, one second after getting out of a bath
- Down the office shredding machine
- Anywhere near a piece of anti-matter
- In the exhaust gases of a space shuttle
- Up your nose, on a first date
- Up your bottom, just before a finger buffet

9 STUPID EXCUSES FOR HAVING A SMALL WILLY

- I've just given blood
- It used to be twice this size. I've just worn it down
- I was a war baby. There was rationing
- It's not mine. I'm on an anatomical exchange scheme with someone from Tokyo
- I was a stunt man in the *Texas Chainsaw Massacre*
- I used to be a really successful gigolo but my accountant advised me to place most of my holding in a tax shelter
- The first eleven are playing away this week
- It shrank in the wash
- This is a latex scaled-down replica. My real one is on temporary loan to the *Guinness Book Of Records* museum

10 ENIGMAS THAT EVEN EINSTEIN COULDN'T SOLVE

- Why ink cartridges for your computer printer cost so much
- Who buys things from The Shopping Channel
- Why people eat Pot Noodles
- Why people you fancy never fancy you
- Where all the money goes
- Why Channel 5 exists
- How the wait in the dentist's can be so long, but life so short...
- Who buys a Crunchie when they can have a Fry's Cream
- Why we like cats
- Why everyone doesn't smash their TV sets whenever Jim Davidson comes on

---

11 OF THE MOST EMBARRASSING TIMES TO PASS WIND

- During the one-minute silence at the Remembrance Day Ceremony
- Live, on *The Time, The Place*
- While proposing
- While delivering a stern lecture on the evils of flatulence in public
- While being knighted by the Queen for services rendered in protecting the environment
- During a televised display of synchronised underwater swimming
- While sitting on your partner's face
- While having an internal examination carried out by two burly customs officers
- During the finals of the 'World Let's See Who

Can Eat Nineteen Boiled Eggs Without Farting'
contest
- During the middle of your delicate haemorrhoid
operation
- When you say 'I do'

---

 11 STUPID WAYS TO TRY TO COMMIT SUICIDE

- Lie blindfolded across the tracks of a model rail-
way (put your fingers in your ears so you can't
hear the train approaching)
- Jump out of a ground-floor window
- Attempt to electrocute yourself with two HP7s
- Douse yourself in Coca Cola and strike a match
- Slash your wrists with a banana
- Throw yourself in front of an oncoming pedal
car driven by your three-year-old niece
- When no one's looking, climb over the railings
of the lemur enclosure at London zoo
- Strap lead weights to your body and jump into
an inflatable paddling pool
- Tie a plastic bag containing loads of big holes
over your head
- Try to OD on blue Smarties
- Develop an unbelievably strong will to live

 **10 PARTS OF THE BODY THAT YOU COULD
QUITE EASILY DO WITHOUT**

- Earlobe
- The dangly thing at the back of your throat
- Hairy moles
- Appendix
- Little toe

- Belly button
- Tonsils
- Armpit hair
- That big spot on your bottom
- Nipples (if you're a man)

---

 10 THINGS BLONDES HAVE – APART FROM MORE FUN

- Blonde hair
- Dark roots
- Dandruff that's harder to spot
- More chance of getting seriously sunburned
- More chance than average of winning a Kim Basinger lookalike contest
- Very little chance of winning a Diana Ross lookalike contest
- A good chance of marrying Rod Stewart (for what that's worth)
- Lots of men automatically assuming they're stupid
- Lots of women automatically assuming they're stupid
- Being the subject of lots of tired old clichés – like 'blondes have more fun'

---

11 SURE SIGNS THAT YOU'RE STARK RAVING MAD

- King Henry II appears by your bedside every night and whispers to you about the cheeses of the world
- You walk into the office one day, stark naked except for one green sock

- You proposed to Derbyshire...
- ...and you told everybody that the saucy minx accepted
- You know you're being followed everywhere by a branch of Debenhams
- You think the government cares about you
- Your sex life revolves around chives and the latest Argos catalogue
- You keep bombarding the BBC with letters to bring back *Doctor Who*
- You change your name by deed poll to 'Winklehoffmeisterbumtittybumtittygonad'
- You dial 0898 numbers...from home
- You actually believe that MFI are genuinely having a '50% off' sale

 10 QUITE APPEALING WAYS TO DIE

- Orgasmed to death by Ulrika Jonsson and Danni Behr
- Overdose on calories after eating twenty servings of chocolate fudge cake and ice cream
- Submerged beneath a tidal wave of Glenlivet and ice
- That's about it, really

 15 OF THE MOST EMBARRASSING THINGS TO ASK FOR IN A CHEMIST

- Their biggest bottle of super-strength acne lotion
- Intimate wipes
- Pile ointment
- Breath freshener

- Diarrhoea medicine
- Panty shields
- Sore-nipple cream
- Bikini-line strip wax
- 'Super Plus' tampons
- Nasal-hair trimmers
- Douche solution
- Flavoured condoms
- 'Extra-Small' condoms
- Anything at all to do with warts
- Anything at all to do with male virility problems

---

 12 STUPID THINGS TO ASK A PLASTIC SURGEON FOR

- A nose like Barbara Streisand's or General Urko's
- A 30AA bust
- Bags under your eyes
- The bits he removed from Michael Jackson, in a box
- Liposuction of the testicles
- A hunchback
- A hairlip
- A club foot
- A face drop
- Ears like Prince Charles
- All the other features of a pencil-necked geek
- A huge bill

THE 11 MOST COMMON OBJECTS REMOVED FROM BODILY ORIFICES ON FRIDAY NIGHT IN THE CASUALTY WARD

- Marrows smeared with taramasalata
- Torches with rubber handles
- Souvenir models of the Eiffel Tower
- Cans of shaving foam (half-empty)
- Umbrellas (half-opened)
- Police truncheons
- Large Toblerones
- Rolled up copies of the *TV Times*
- Gerbils
- Sticks of rock
- Fists (still attached to their rather sheepish-looking owners)

12 STUPID MEDICAL CONDITIONS YOU WOULDN'T WANT TO GET

- Impotence of a severity that the medical profession has never known but which is so interesting that all the medical students in Europe are coached in to look at you and point
- Something you caught from your wife that you thought only your best friend had
- Incontinence of Trevi Fountain-like proportions
- Unexplainable distortion of the facial muscles that make you look like Mick Hucknell's dad
- Developing a sudden unexplainable allergy to everything
- Anything that involves a plaster cast of your misshapen genitalia being put on permanent display in the foyer of Guy's Teaching Hospital
- Growing a third (nipple on your forehead)

- Leprosy of the testes
- Anything that requires a team of top proctologists to fly in from Budapest to perform an emergency operation immediately
- Anything where, after the operation, the surgeon tells you that, to save your little toe, they had to amputate your penis
- A new strain of pubic lice that's resistant to anything except light artillery
- Turet's Syndrome (your favourite karaoke song will come out as 'I did it piss piss arseholes my toss wank way')

 12 THINGS THAT ARE BAD FOR YOU

- A bucket of Polish vodka
- Throwing yourself head first into a live volcano
- BSE-infected salmonella
- Wayward women
- Married men
- Radioactive suppositories
- Running into an anthrax lab and doing deep-breathing exercises
- Shagging the girlfriend of a heavyweight boxer
- Consuming eighty cheeseburgers in half as many minutes
- The working week
- Anything you enjoy
- Death

21 STUPID THINGS TO BELIEVE YOU'LL EVER BE

- Happy

- Younger
- Thinner
- Married to Alicia Silverstone (and cheating on her with Kate Winslet)
- Rich
- Purple
- Still alive in the year 2100
- A frog
- Respected
- Listened to
- Influential
- A beer taster for British Steel
- Lime-flavoured
- Jeremy Beadle
- Your own brother
- Given proper medical care on the NHS
- Reincarnated
- Successful
- A railway train
- Invited to an orgy
- Safe

---

15 STUPID PLACES TO RELIEVE YOURSELF

- Over the TV in your living room
- In a box at the Royal Opera House
- In a crowded lift
- In an empty, but glass-walled, lift
- Directly on to exposed power cables
- Over your boss's car
- Over your boss
- Live on national television
- On the desk at your job interview
- In the confessional
- In the font at a christening

- Over a neighbour's dog – in an act of revenge...
- In the supermarket's chill cabinet
- In your car while trying a tricky overtaking manoeuvre
- All over the Union Jack tattoo on the beefiest skinhead you can find

---

 12 STUPID EXAMPLES OF BODY LANGUAGE GUARANTEED NOT TO ATTRACT ANYONE OF THE OPPOSITE SEX

- Picking your nose but trying to make it look like you're scratching it
- Picking your nose but trying to make it look like you're squeezing a blackhead
- Getting that annoying bit of earwax out of your ear with a biro
- Scratching your crotch frantically
- Nodding constantly and smiling inanely
- Trying to touch your left ear with your right hand, over the top of your head
- Sucking your toes
- Doing your 'hilarious' impression of the Robo Cop walk
- Holding your breath until you pass out
- Going cross-eyed on purpose
- Thrusting your stomach out as far as it will go
- Plunging your finger in and out of your mouth with that knowing look

---

 10 THINGS YOU SHOULD DEFINITELY INSIST ON WHEN YOU HAVE A VASECTOMY

- Anaesthetic

- Sterilised equipment
- A surgeon who doesn't bear a grudge against you
- A surgeon who's a real surgeon and not some loony in a white coat who wandered into the hospital off the street
- A surgeon who's done this operation before
- Only having the operation you went in for (e.g. not a sex change at the same time)
- A fresh scalpel
- The operation taking place in a proper operating theatre and not on a table in the staff canteen surrounded by half a dozen old cups of coffee and a sticky bun
- A surgeon who doesn't suffer from epilepsy
- Proper neat little stitches, not rivets, staples or a big bulldog clip

11 STUPID THINGS THAT ARE MARGINALLY LESS PAINFUL THAN NATURAL CHILDBIRTH

- Getting Dawn French to stand on your foot
- Getting a paper cut in the little bit of webbed skin between your fingers and then pouring lemon juice over it
- Slamming your fingers in the front door
- Pouring boiling hot water through a funnel down your trousers
- Having your nipples pierced with a blunt pencil
- Feeding your feet into a paper shredder
- Rolling naked in a clump of stinging nettles
- Sticking a knitting needle in your eye
- Eating a cactus
- Having a full body wax by a beauty therapist who's new to the job
- Having a red-hot poker rammed up your bottom

Day by day

---

 25 STUPID THINGS YOU'LL ALWAYS FIND IN YOUR LOCAL STREET MARKET

- A video stall with 400 copies of *Carry on Sergeant* and a range of horror films so dire even your local video shop wouldn't stock them
- Electrical goods withdrawn from sale as unsafe eighteen months ago
- Brightly coloured toxic children's toys and jumbo fun colouring books with only five pages in them
- Someone the police are looking for
- A stall with nothing you could ever possibly want on it
- Pickpockets
- The place where your mum buys your socks
- Runner-up, three years running, in the 'short-changer of the year' contest
- Leather jackets in all the latest seventies styles (as seen on *The Sweeney*)
- Someone who pretends he doesn't speak any English when you ask for your money back
- Someone else the police are looking for
- Cheap packets of Mr Kipling pies, bleached by the sun and 'on the turn'
- Enticingly priced bootleg tapes of top-thirty albums which turn out to be blank when you get them home

- Half the things you lost when you were last burgled
- The bloke who sold you the falafel that had you in bed for two months
- A chocolate-misshape emporium
- T-shirts with Posh Spice on them (at least until you iron them)
- Display of wicked-looking flick knives and bayonets
- Dud-battery stall
- A stray Doberman eating squashed fruit off the floor and eyeing up pushchairs
- A transit van blocking the main access road
- A fight
- A hamburger-van-cum-mobile-toilet
- A stall selling cheese that smells like Jono Alumo's crotch
- Packets of sweet cigarettes, still on sale fifteen years after they were withdrawn

---

 10 STUPID NEW YEAR RESOLUTIONS

- Take up smoking
- Try to halve your salary
- Put on 84lbs
- Breathe only once every forty seconds
- Assassinate a foreign dignitary
- Put chocolate biscuits down your underwear every day for the whole year
- Sell your new car for £3.50
- Spend less time with your family
- Learn to recite the Koran in fluent Turkish
- Take this stupid book back to the shop

✳ 10 STUPID ADVANTAGES OF BEING THREE FEET TALL

- You can save money by wearing children's clothes (but then again, who wants to go through life wearing sailors' outfits or blue velvet pinafore dresses with lace collars?)
- If a bullet was coming towards you four feet off the ground, it would miss you easily
- You're twice as tall as someone who's only 1' 6" tall
- You're a veritable giant amongst men compared with people who are only 1' tall
- You can head-butt bullies in the nuts
- You can look through keyholes without stooping
- You can get your identical twin to stand on your shoulders, cover yourselves with a long coat and get into an eighteen certificate film
- If you're destitute you only need a small cardboard box to live in
- If you're writing a dissertation on 'The Smell Of People's Crotches', you're perfectly placed to do your research
- You're virtually guaranteed a part in *Snow White II: The Adventure Continues*

15 THINGS THAT SEEM TO GO ON FOR EVER

- The working day
- Visits from relatives
- Train journeys in carriages packed with drunken football fans
- Your time in the dentist's chair
- The wait between erections

- Exams you haven't revised for
- The wait before you get your exam results
- Your Barclaycard statement
- Twenty consecutive 99-year prison sentences
- The trailers on a video before the main film starts
- 'Bohemian Rhapsody'
- Correspondence with your insurance company
- Televised snooker tournaments
- Sexual intercourse with either one of the authors
- Infinity

9 THINGS THAT ALWAYS SEEM TO END TOO SOON

- A ride on the dodgems
- An erection
- The latest episode of *The Simpsons*
- Your last relationship
- Sleep
- That pack of E-180 videos you bought
- Lunch breaks
- Fifteen minutes of fame
- Life

14 OTHER THINGS, APART FROM PRIDE, THAT COME BEFORE A FALL

- Copious amounts of alcohol
- Some swine, loosening the screws on a hand rail
- Investing your life savings in stocks and shares
- An unwise venture on to a ledge

- Trying to take photos of Liam Gallagher when he doesn't want you to
- A daredevil game of hopscotch on a parapet
- Entering 'Amateur Tightrope Walker of the Year'
- Vanessa Feltz climbing on your shoulders shouting, 'Piggy back! Piggy back!'
- An impromptu tango on a roller coaster
- A lightning-fast strike by highly trained trampoline thieves
- Having an unexplained impulse to cover your whole kitchen floor with margarine
- Sticking your knob into a White House intern's mouth
- A special offer on roller blades for the over-sixties
- Betting your mate you can wing walk on an F-16

 9 STUPID THINGS YOU'LL ALWAYS FIND IN A PUBLIC TOILET

- A strategically placed spy hole through to the next cubicle
- Pervy and disgusting graffiti on the inside of the door that you feel compelled to read, even though you're repulsed
- A lone turd, floating
- Cheap toilet paper that's either abrasive or greasy
- Cigarette burns on the edge of the seat or on the top of the hot-air dryers
- An unidentified substance on the handle that you discover by accident only when you come to flush

- A lock that doesn't
- A puddle of a strange, yet familiar-smelling liquid on the tiles
- Roller towels designed so that 78 people use the same two-foot length of linen

---

✳ 10 STUPID THINGS YOU WON'T FIND IN A TYPICAL AMISH HOUSEHOLD

- A multiplay CD system and the whole set of Guns 'n' Roses albums
- A huge poster of Pamela Anderson
- An Uzi
- Cocaine with a street value of $600,000
- The keys to a supercharged Pontiac Trans Am
- 27 back issues of *Playboy*, some with 'water damage'
- A wardrobe full of bright, skimpy beachwear
- A fridge crammed full of Bud
- Edible underwear
- A bottle of strawberry-flavoured 'Joy-Jelly'

✳ 11 STUPID WAYS TO RAISE THE DEVIL

- Look under 'D' in the phone book
- Put a postcard headed 'Wanted' in the newsagent's window
- Go into a police station and ask to look through their mug shots
- Play your Chris de Burgh records backwards and listen for a hidden message
- Play your Chris de Burgh records the right way and listen for a hidden message
- Scour the streets of a nice neighbourhood on a

sunny day
- Draw a pentangle on the ground – then run away
- Sacrifice an ant on a black marble altar
- Sit cross-legged in a dark room filled with incense, close your eyes, concentrate and slowly chant 'Come out, come out, wherever you are'
- Slam your fingers in your car door
- Ask Cilla on *Surprise, Surprise* to reunite you with him

---

 16 STUPID THINGS WE BET YOU'VE ALWAYS WANTED TO DO

- Walk up a 'down' escalator
- Drive your car on purpose into the asshole that just cut you up
- Grope the person next to you on a crowded train
- Carry a big gun
- Answer a lonely-hearts ad
- Hide in a department store and then wander around it alone after closing time
- Pose for a nudie mag
- Shoplift
- Kick a skinhead right in the bollocks
- Join the five-mile-high club
- Photocopy your bottom
- Measure your willie
- Have an affair
- Nob the entire female cast of *Cats*
- Hold up a security van
- Tell the boss what a wanker he is

☀ 11 STUPID THINGS TO TAKE INTO THE SHOWER WITH YOU

- Any substance that gives off toxic gases when in contact with water
- The end of a live mains cable
- Three people selected at random from the phone book
- A prize-winning sculpture, carved out of a solid block of salt
- A jellyfish
- A Picasso ink drawing that you've just bought at an auction
- A BBC1 film crew making a documentary about plankton
- A shampoo bottle containing industrial-strength bleach
- Soap in the shape of something suggestive which might tempt you to spend longer in the shower than is healthy for you
- The Olympic torch
- 3000 Alka Seltzers without wrappers

---

11 STUPID THINGS TO CARRY IN YOUR HANDBAG

- Your boyfriend, because he's tired of walking
- Any other form of dead weight
- A piece of Edam cheese – just in case you get attacked
- A street map of Zagreb
- A photograph of Ed 'Stewpot' Stewart
- Used toilet tissue
- Volume VI of the *Encyclopaedia Britannica*
- £20,000 in 20p pieces

- A used condom, so he can prove just how much he really desires you
- The contents of a neighbour's wheelie bin
- Two pounds of fluid jelly you're waiting to set

 WHAT YOUR BEST FRIEND SAYS (AND WHAT SHE REALLY MEANS)

- That look is really you (Cheap, uncoordinated and trashy)
- Of course it suits you (You always look that rough)
- I won't tell a soul, cross my heart (Where's my telephone book?)
- Of course it's not too small (You're just too large)
- Of course it's not too revealing (I can't wait to see their faces!)
- I wouldn't be telling you this if I weren't your friend (And didn't enjoy stirring it)
- Perhaps I shouldn't be telling you this... (I can't wait to tell you this!)
- Maybe marriage will change him... (I give the two of you six months, tops)
- No one will ever guess (Until I tell them, that is)
- You look fabulous! (Tarty cow...)
- It's just what I've always wanted! (You wait until your birthday...)
- Will you take a friendly word of advice... (Or twenty minutes of calculated, vitriolic, malicious, catty criticism masquerading as advice?)
- Why don't you give him another chance? (The last time was soooooo funny)
- You look like the perfect couple... (Laurel and Hardy)

- Goodness knows what it must have cost you! (£12.99 including VAT – which is half what I spent on you, you cow!)
- I just don't know how he found out (Unless me telling him had anything to do with it)
- I love those jeans on you (Because they accentuate your child-bearing hips)
- Everybody goes through it (If they're chronically plain and dull, that is...)
- That's the perfect dress for you! (I can't be bothered to go back to all the other shops)

---

 12 UNSUITABLE TOPICS OF CONVERSATION AT A DINNER PARTY

- Rigor mortis
- Enemas
- The dog's boil
- Your boil
- Ethiopia
- Where the stuff between your toes comes from
- How ugly the hostess is
- Precisely how the animal on your plate was slaughtered
- Where exactly the vas deferens is to be found
- Your strange habit of spitting in any food you cook
- Glass eyes
- The high local incidence of burglary when couples go out to dinner parties

28 THINGS YOU'VE PROBABLY GOT IN YOUR HANDBAG RIGHT THIS VERY MINUTE

- A crumpled Danielle Steel paperback
- Some loose change
- Lipstick
- Make-up mirror
- A quarter of a packet of stale Polos
- A disposable lighter (empty)
- Hairspray
- A crumpled up clipping from a problem page
- A crumpled up, used Kleenex smeared with make-up
- A crumpled photo of your boyfriend
- A crumpled photo of your parents
- A powder compact
- A book of matches from a restaurant
- A phone number you jotted down, but can't remember whose
- A huge bunch of keys on a stupid novelty key ring
- Two unpaid bills
- Half an old chocolate bar covered with fluff
- Credit-card counterfoils
- The cap from an eyeliner pencil
- A nail file
- One stick of Juicy Fruit
- Three loose tampons
- A dirty hairbrush
- Assorted receipts
- A purse
- A torn-out recipe you'll never make
- A diary you hardly ever use
- Old tangerine peel squashed down into one corner

✳ 12 UPDATED SAYINGS

- It's not the winning that counts, it's the bung you get for throwing the match
- Red sky at night, arsonists at the B&Q warehouse
- A fool and his money should watch out for fitted-kitchen salesmen
- Smile, and the world thinks you're simple
- People in glass houses should watch out for vandals
- Act in haste, end up with a crap pension
- Look before you buy double glazing
- A rolling stone is exceedingly rich
- A bird in the hand guarantees a great Friday night
- Children should be seen because then you know they're not lifting your car stereo
- The devil finds use for white-van drivers
- Too many cooks are on TV at the moment

✳ 12 THINGS THAT ARE MORE EXPENSIVE THAN YOU THINK

- A Solero ice lolly
- A cup of tea at The Ritz
- A return rail ticket to Liverpool
- Your car's 12,000-mile service
- Dental treatment
- A new pair of jeans
- Two tickets to the theatre
- Having your shoes repaired
- A second-hand Volkswagen Golf
- A baby
- Living in London
- CDs

16 STUPID THINGS YOU REGRET DOING – BUT STILL DO

- Scratching it
- Falling in love
- Catching diseases
- Going to a local amateur-dramatics production
- Buying those ridiculous shoes
- Working for that utter pig...
- Reading the new James Herbert novel
- Buying that giant-sized Mars Bar
- Eating that giant-sized Mars Bar
- Getting up in the morning
- Dyeing your hair that colour
- Leaving your Christmas shopping to the last possible minute
- Having that one last drink
- Forgetting someone's birthday
- Buying expensive electrical goods, which you know full well aren't going to last as long as a typical British summer...
- Swatting poor harmless spiders crawling up the side of the bath tub

---

8 STUPID THINGS TO DO IN THE CLOTHES SHOP

- Put all the size 10 dresses on size 14 hangers
- Ask the shop assistant if you can have a dress like hers, only two sizes smaller
- Wait until someone picks up a dress and heads for the changing room. Pick up an identical dress in the smallest size available and then follow her in. While she's undressing, swop the dresses over

- If someone asks you to do them up at the back, pretend to be violently struggling. Dig your knee into the small of her back and tug at the zip, puffing and panting. Say, 'I'll have to go and get a shoe horn' – and leave
- Ask the shop assistant for a dress like hers, only one that fits properly
- Find the most revolting dress in the entire shop and start enthusing about how trendy and exciting it is. Wait until the stampede for it starts and then slip out of the shop
- While someone is busy trying on a swimsuit, pick up all her discarded clothing, walk out, hand it to the assistant and say, 'No thanks. You can put them back now.'
- When someone asks you to help them on with a dress, run a stanley knife down the seam. Tell her to cross her arms to make sure it fits

 ## 18 STUPID AND HEARTLESS THINGS TO SAY IN A COMMUNAL CHANGING ROOM

- That's a bit expensive just for a dare, isn't it?
- Excuse me, but have you seen the back of your knicks?
- I saw a dress just like that one in Woolworth's yesterday.
- Hey! Get out of here you filthy pervert! – Oh, I'm sorry. I thought you were a man...
- I had a dress like that. My boyfriend made me throw it away because he said it made me look like Edna Everage
- Pardon me, but I think that will clash terribly with your spots...
- Excuse me, but would you stop staring at me? Yes...you...

- Look, if you're that desperate to attract a man I'll fix you up myself...
- Excuse me for asking, but you seem to know something I don't. Is the 'Plain, severe and drab' look in this season?
- I'd get some acne cream to go with that backless dress if I were you
- Size 12? That's a bit optimistic, isn't it?
- Hi, I'm from Weightwatchers...
- I wouldn't buy that dress if I were you. All it does is accentuate your roots.
- God, you'll have to shave those legs if you want to wear that...
- Excuse me, but since you're obviously colour blind would you like any help?
- Isn't it funny how some clothes just accentuate the tummy like that?
- God, you're fat. Don't you care about yourself?
- I'm sorry. I owe you an apology. I'm the store detective. I followed you in here because I thought you'd stuffed six dresses, four skirts and a raincoat up your jumper, but I can see now that it's really all you...

☀ 10 THINGS YOU DON'T WANT TO SEE FIRST THING IN THE MORNING

- That half-drained bottle of whisky from the night before
- The alarm clock telling you it's 10.30...
- Yourself in the mirror
- Dried spew in your partner's hair (which you know you'll have to tell them about...)
- The washing-up you left in the sink, in the hope that it would somehow do itself

- A big rip in the condom you dumped on the bedside cabinet
- The remains of the Chinese takeaway all over the coffee table
- Lorraine Kelly on breakfast telly
- Yesterday's contraceptive pill, next to the glass of water...
- What the dog did in the night...

 10 CHARITIES YOU'D HAVE TO BE STUPID TO MAKE DONATIONS TO

- Save the Cockroach
- The 'Shoot the Elderly' Campaign
- The Distressed Nazi Gentlefolk Association
- The Prince of Wales Appeal for better skiing conditions in Klosters
- The 'Help the Rich and Privileged' Campaign
- Famine Relief for Switzerland
- Shotgun Aid (helping to keep blood-sports enthusiasts armed and ready!)
- Sponsored Giant Panda Eating
- The 'Donate your Kidneys to Rich Arabs in Harley Street Clinics' Appeal
- The Moonies

Law and order

9 STUPID ALTERNATIVES TO THE ELECTRIC CHAIR

- The steam sofa
- The gas stool
- The solar lounger
- The wave-powered scatter cushion
- The clockwork ottoman
- The internal-combustion bean bag
- The hydro-electric hammock
- The cold-fusion chaise longue
- The atomic three-piece suite

10 STUPID PEOPLE TO PHONE WHEN YOU'RE TAKEN INTO POLICE CUSTODY

- The solicitor who represents the Police Federation
- The solicitor who represented Ian Brady, Dennis Nilsen, Lester Piggot and The Guinness Four
- Pizzaland
- The one person you don't want to know about your arrest

- The talking clock
- International Rescue
- Your local newspaper, so you can get maximum embarrassment from your ordeal
- Dyno-Rod
- Commissioner Gordon
- Yourself (even though you know you're not home)

---

10 STUPID THINGS TO DEMAND DURING A BANK ROBBERY

- £25,000 in one-pence pieces
- £25,000 in marked bills
- A cheque for £25,000 made payable to yourself
- £5
- That you be locked in the vault and the police called
- A fluorescent-green Reliant Robin as a getaway car
- Shorter working hours for people in the haberdashery business
- Anything beginning with 'X' (including a xantippe and a xebec)
- The location of El Dorado
- That only your good side be filmed on the hidden security cameras

---

10 STUPID THINGS TO SAY TO A POLICEMAN

- Oi, pig!
- That photofit on *Crimestoppers* was me!
- Of course I've been drinking...
- Here's £3.50 to forget all about it

- Keep watch while I throw ammonia in the guard's face
- Your helmet looks like a giant prick
- Psssst! Interested in a Sony Nicam video recorder for sixty quid?
- I've got six ounces of illegal substances concealed up my arse
- You'll never take me alive, copper!
- I wish to make an official complaint about a police officer

 10 THINGS YOU DON'T NORMALLY ASSOCIATE WITH HIGH COURT JUDGES

- The song 'Young, Gifted and Black'
- Muscles
- Feminism
- Trendiness
- Indifference when it comes to young boys in tight trousers
- Comprehensive-school education
- Body piercing
- Fingers on pulses
- Sexual behaviour that can in any way be called 'normal'
- Justice

 8 PEOPLE YOU DON'T WANT TO FIND YOURSELF SHARING A CELL WITH

- Some homicidal maniac who's violently claustrophobic
- Some hard nut who says you remind him of his girlfriend

- Some pervert who says you remind him of his dog
- Some head case who says you remind him of his toilet
- Anyone called Beefy Steve
- Anyone called Part-Them-Buns Benny
- Dr Hannibal Lector
- Matthew Corbett (in case he has a dream where he thinks you're Sooty)

---

 11 REALLY, REALLY STUPID CONSPIRACY THEORIES*

- All the Apollo moon landings were faked. They were actually filmed on the beach at Bournemouth while no one was looking
- Kennedy was assassinated because he knew the formula for the secret herbs and spices used to flavour Kentucky Fried Chicken (witnesses say they saw a 'Southern gentleman with a short goatee beard' running away from the Texas Book Depository)
- Jim Morrison faked his own death so he could re-invent himself as Chris de Burgh (If you drop an 'R', his name is an anagram of 'I Jism Moron', which proves it)
- Black helicopters do exist. They're there to film bad drivers so footage can be used on *Police Camera Action*
- The third Fatima prophecy reveals that Bruce Forsyth is the anti-Christ and Armageddon will begin during the ad break in the 666th episode of *Play Your Cards Right*
- Space aliens run Mothercare for their own nefarious purposes

- Einstein's brain was removed after death and preserved in the US Government's top-secret vault for storing 'Things that make you queasy when you look at them'
- Elvis isn't dead. He's being frozen until future scientists find a cure for being a 'dumb Southern redneck'
- Nothing happens at Area 51. All the action is next door at Area 52
- Hitler was cloned by Nazi scientists and is now the Uruguayan national soccer team
- The world is secretly run by the people we vote for
  *or are they...

---

10 STUPID WAYS TO DISGUISE YOURSELF PRIOR TO COMMITTING A CRIMINAL ACT

- Change your shoes
- Wear your coat inside out
- Smear yourself with boot polish (or whitewash)
- Wear a striped jersey and carry a sack with 'swag' stencilled on it
- Wear a basque instead of a mask
- Slash your face with a razor to create a prominent scar
- Cut off an arm so police will think that a one-armed man committed the crime (which he did)
- Dress up as the Pope, because no one will suspect the Pope of committing a crime
- Wear a giant penguin suit, so that police will be convinced witnesses are mistaken (or just mental)
- Disguise yourself as yourself, so that you can claim you were framed

10 STUPID WAYS TO TRY TO BECOME THE TOTALLY RUTHLESS, UNDISPUTED MASTER OF THE WORLD

- Ask nicely
- Find a steady job, be conscientious and dedicated, and hope to work your way up through the ranks to Master of the World
- Try to take over the world when nobody's looking
- Tell everyone that you're the Master of the World – and hope they believe you
- Threaten to have a temper tantrum unless you get world power
- Make a cash offer for it
- Disguise yourself as Master of the World – and hope no one looks too closely
- Attempt to win the world in a lottery
- Replace all the world leaders with android doubles who are under your complete control
- Marry the Totally Ruthless, Undisputed Mistress of the World

---

 10 STUPID LAST REQUESTS ON DEATH ROW

- To hear 'Wombling Merry Christmas' one last time
- To have something from Spud-U-Like as your last meal
- To go three hours early
- To make a dinner reservation for next weekend
- To sleep with Barbara Cartland
- To consult a life-insurance salesman
- To visit the dentist
- To have Sir Harry Secombe's autograph

- To meet Rolf Harris in the flesh
- A calendar

9 THINGS HIGH COURT JUDGES DON'T USUALLY LISTEN TO

- Radio One
- *Thomas the Tank Engine Stories*, read by Ringo Starr
- Motley Crue
- Stupid women
- Doctors who told them fifteen years ago that their brains were going
- That small voice inside that says 'You're talking nonsense
- Their hearts
- Public opinion
- Reason

8 PEOPLE NOT TO NOMINATE AS A CHARACTER WITNESS

- Charles Manson
- Your six-month-old nephew
- Anyone suffering from amnesia
- Someone who hates you
- Someone who you've never met before in your life
- Someone you don't ever want to be associated with
- Anyone who's going to want a huge cash sum for helping you out
- Anyone who's going to claim that you bribed them with a huge cash sum for helping you out

The **Amazing** world of confectionery

 13 STUPID NAMES FOR SWEETS THAT DON'T EXIST BUT, IF THEY DID, YOU'D BE VERY EMBARRASSED ASKING FOR THEM

- Wobbly Bobblies
- Chocolate Bottoms
- Zitties
- Williemints
- Knickie Knackie Knooes
- Noblet Crunch
- Whizzleybums
- Spunky Pieces
- Raspberry Nobends
- Crunchy Bumwipes
- Fatty-Fatty Gobble Bars
- Hitler Chews
- Nutty Pus Creams

10 STUPID THINGS TO DO WITH A BIG BAR OF CHOCOLATE

- Throw it in the bin
- Unwrap it, smear it with axle grease and then give it to a loved one
- Eat half, then offer to sell it back to the shop for half the price you bought it for (minus a 10% handling charge)
- Eat half, then send it back to the manufacturer claiming a manufacturing defect
- Smear it all over your face and pretend to be six months old
- Melt it down and use it as yummy eye shadow
- Use it as a smear-on deodorant
- Take your shoes and socks off and jump up and down on it, to make your feet look dirtier than they really are
- Give the dog a bite before you take one
- Save it so you can celebrate the millennium in style

---

10 STUPID SETS OF BUBBLE GUM-CARDS YOU WOULDN'T BOTHER TO COLLECT

- Soccer Stars' Brothers
- Eminent Belgian Ear, Nose and Throat Specialists
- Colours of the Rainbow
- Shoes of the Kings and Queens of England
- Breakfast-TV Cameramen
- Complex Equations and Formulae
- Stars of Shinty
- Wimbledon Champions with Their Backs to the Camera

- Prominent Members of Local Government (turn them over to form a giant 36 x 18 inch picture of the head of Elmbridge Borough Council)
- Famous People with Nosebleeds

---

 16 STUPID FLAVOURS YOU MIGHT EXPECT TO FIND IN A BOX OF 'QUALITY STREET LAXATIVE ASSORTMENT'

- Bowelbuster Cluster
- Caramel Pooh Supreme
- Leaky Orange Dream
- Strawberry Gush Nightmare
- Hazelnut Anal Catharsis Whirl
- Sugar-Coated Almond Dumpies
- Marzipan Turd Purge Royale
- Coconut Intestinal Screaming Abdabs
- Montelimar Shitstreamer
- Coffee Bottom Terror
- Sphincter Surprise
- Truffle Plop DeLuxe
- Noisette Ringpiece Demolisher
- Lime Trouser Torment
- Steamy Lemon Bogsquatter
- Cherry Shitemeister

Fame
and fortune

 13 WORDS HARDLY EVER – OR NEVER – USED TO DESCRIBE TONY BLAIR

- Insectivoid
- Female
- Shuttlecock
- Principled
- Thrilling
- Tasty
- Oblong
- Scrumptious
- Muscley
- Edible
- Nobtastic
- Fluorescent
- Socialist

 10 STUPID THINGS (APART FROM ORANGE JUICE) THAT O. J. SIMPSON'S FIRST TWO INITIALS COULD STAND FOR

- Oblivious Jock
- Overdeveloped Juvenile
- Objectionably Jammy
- Obvious Jailbird

- Overly Jealous
- Offensive Jerk
- Organ Jabber
- Open Jugular
- Out-to-lunch Jury
- Octopus Jehovah

---

5 WORDS JIM DAVIDSON PROBABLY CAN'T PRONOUNCE, LET ALONE UNDERSTAND

- Misogynist
- Irascible
- Magnanimous
- Obtuse
- Sobriety

---

10 STUPID PLACES WE BET YOU WON'T FIND ELVIS PRESLEY

- Under your bed
- Serving behind the cheese counter in your local Sainsbury's
- Impersonating himself in local amateur-talent contests
- Sitting opposite you when you travel to work next Monday morning
- In a rehearsal studio preparing for his comeback tour
- In a keep-fit class in heaven
- Orbiting the earth in a Soviet space station
- In a top-secret hideaway along with Jim Morrison
- In cryogenic suspension waiting for the day when science finally finds an antidote to

'Stuffing Your Face With Cheeseburgers'
- Alive

---

12 FAMOUS PEOPLE WITH RUDE NAMES

- Urethra Franklin
- Epididymis Bosch
- Sir Arthur Colon Doyle
- J. Arthur Wank
- Mark Twat
- Jackson Bollock
- Edgar Allen Pooh
- Charles Dickend
- Jean-Paul Fartre
- William Shatner
- e e cummings
- Tony Hancock

---

9 THINGS THE SPICE GIRLS REALLY, REALLY WANT

- Wit
- Charm
- The return of those Polaroids
- Sophistication
- Elegance
- Talent
- More than just rudimentary intelligence
- An end to the rumours that they'll split up in 1998
- Not to be the butt of cheap jibes in humour books

13 NICKNAMES THE ELEPHANT MAN HAD TO ENDURE AT SCHOOL

- Floppy Skin
- Repugno
- Trunky
- Big Head
- Nellie
- Pachyderm Features
- Jumbo Bonce
- Deformo
- Snorky Jack
- Tusker
- Mutie Merrick
- Jumbo John
- Mo Mowlam

6 GREEK PHILOSOPHERS WHO WERE ALSO RAPPERS

- L.L. Cool Socrates
- Ice T. Plato
- M.C. Aristotle
- The Ranking Mr Pythagoras
- Grandmaster Diogenes and his Furious Five
- Run Pericles

16 STUPID THINGS THAT WOULD HAPPEN IF A PENGUIN BECAME PRIME MINISTER

- Things could only get better
- It would make a refreshing change from the usual dodos
- There'd be bird droppings all over the carpets of

10 Downing Street

- The Queen's Speech would be full of references to fish and jumping off rocks
- We'd enjoy the best diplomatic relations with Antarctica in 200 years
- The Prime Minister's chair in the cabinet room would have to be lowered considerably
- There would be a lot of squawking during Prime Minister's question time
- Great Britain would declare war on sea lions
- The Prime Minister could avoid awkward issues by not understanding what was going on, rather than by lying and conniving
- The 'Prime Minister cuddly toy' industry would recover from the doldrums it's been in ever since the Clement Attlee debacle
- There'd be no question of selling out the Falklands
- Short people would feel better represented in Parliament
- And so would small flightless birds
- Jeremy Paxman would get his nose bitten for asking an impertinent question
- Crowds would flock to see 'Prime Minister's feeding time' every day at 4.30 p.m.
- Everyone would be relieved it wasn't William Hague

 11 FAMOUS PEOPLE YOU NEVER KNEW SLEPT TOGETHER

- Mao Tse Tung and Cleo Laine
- Pablo Picasso and Su Pollard
- Marilyn Monroe and Sir Alf Ramsey
- Norman Wisdom and Elle MacPherson

- Rock Hudson and Liberace
- Queen Victoria, Gordon of Khartoum and Charles Darwin
- Pope John Paul and Diana Dors
- Florence Nightingale and The 4th Light Durham Infantry
- Albert Einstein and Gracie Fields
- Fatty Arbuckle and Rin Tin Tin
- Admiral Nelson and Joan Collins

 17 MARX BROTHERS WHO NEVER MADE IT...

(Everyone knows Groucho, Chico and Harpo; devoted fans will probably have heard of Zeppo and Gummo, who made rare appearances in Marx Brothers' films – but hardly anyone knows about the other brothers who never made it into the movies...)

- Leppo
- Vommo
- Sucko
- Pricko
- Sypho
- Lino
- Incontinento
- Ringo
- Crossdressero
- Homo
- Flatulo
- Typhoido
- Nobbo
- Pervo
- Fellatio
- Thicko
- Sumo

12 STUPID THINGS YOU NEVER KNEW ABOUT THE TELETUBBIES

- Tinky Winky once worked as Christopher Biggin's stunt double
- The Noo-noo has been romantically linked with Princess Stephanie of Monaco
- Teletubby sex is unique in the animal kingdom. To reproduce they simply pay more Equity members to put on costumes...
- Po hasn't got a licence for that TV set in her stomach
- They smell like old sick
- Dipsy drinks
- There were five of them, but one got eaten by a shark
- Laa-Laa is often mistaken for Vanessa Feltz
- Po changed her name from Wanko-Shatz on the producer's advice
- They're cannibals
- 'Eh Oh' is very, very rude...
- They're highly inflammable

THE GREAT PHILOSOPHERS' FAVOURITE BISCUITS

- Epicurus ('After tasting them, I would have to say Bourbons')
- Jeremy Bentham ('I usually have whatever everyone else is having')
- David Hume ('It is not actually ever possible to truly know which is your favourite biscuit')
- Jean-Jacques Rousseau ('Anything with no artificial preservatives and flavourings')
- Thomas Hobbes ('Chocolate Hob-Nobs! Do you

want a fight about it?')
- René Descartes ('I like both Viscounts and Jammy Dodgers')
- Benedict de Spinoza ('I agree with Descartes about the Viscounts, but not about the Jammy Dodgers')
- Blaise Pascal ('I like whatever biscuit God thinks is nicest; that way, if He exists, He won't be offended at my choice of biscuit')
- Auguste Compte ('After taking a thoroughly scientific approach to the question, I have come to the conclusion that it is Ginger Nuts')
- Bertrand Russell ('I took the same approach, but for my money, it's Huntley & Palmer's Butter Biscuits')
- Jean-Paul Sartre (To say one has a favourite biscuit is to admit the choice is purely subjective and that we cannot objectively say that one biscuit is any better than any other')
- Arthur Schopenhauer ('I don't care')
- Friedrich Nietzsche ('Garibaldis are the Uberbiscuit and tomorrow belongs to them!')

 THE REAL NAMES OF FAMOUS MOVIE STARS

- John Wayne (Marion Botty)
- Kirk Douglas (Ricky Dibble)
- Rudolph Valentino (Harry Sick)
- Humphrey Bogart (Dennis Snotrag)
- Orson Welles (Prince the Wonder Dog)
- Alan Ladd (Ernest Borgnine)
- Cary Grant (Archibald Leech)
- Ernest Borgnine (Alan Ladd)
- Cyd Charisse (Sid Charise)
- Judy Garland (Francis Gumm)

- Alec Guinness (Alec Light-Ale)
- Marlon Brando (Marlon Stott)
- Zsa Zsa Gabor (Doris Smedley)
- Norman Wisdom (Norman Stupid)
- Rod Steiger (Sheik Abdullah al Rahmani of Qatar)
- Burt Reynolds (Debbie Reynolds)
- Anthony Quinn (Pope Gregory XIV)
- Joseph Bottoms (Clint Sphincter)
- Ginger Rogers (Ginger Buggery)

 WINSTON CHURCHILL'S ALL-TIME FAVOURITE HATS

- Bowler
- Panama
- Stetson
- Beret
- Fez
- Turban
- Pork Pie

---

 7 STUPID DEFINITIONS OF FREUDIAN CONCEPTS

- OEDIPUS COMPLEX: a modern art gallery in Paris just around the corner from the Pompidou Centre
- LATENCY: closet homosexuality
- REPRESSION: chief feature of the Sandinista regime
- ELECTRA COMPLEX: Luton's answer to the Plaza shopping centre
- AUTO EROTICISM: The car as a penis substitute
- LIBIDO: where you go to swim and sail boats

The gracious world of Royalty

 10 WORDS AND PHRASES THAT YOU'LL NEVER HEAR IN THE QUEEN'S CHRISTMAS SPEECH

- Git
- Nice to see you, to see you, nice
- I bet my TV set is better than the one you're watching on...
- So there I was, naked as the day I was born...
- Smack my bitch up
- Plebian Scum
- Of course, hereditary madness runs in our family...
- Did you hear the one about...
- So I urge you all to storm the Palace and instigate a revolution
- Sorry

8 PEOPLE WHO SOUND LIKE THEY MAY BE RELATIVES OF THE QUEEN (BUT AREN'T)

- Prince Naseem Hamed
- Count Basie
- Jack Lord
- Martin Luther King
- Duke Ellington
- Steve McQueen
- The Baron Knights
- Dame Edna Everage

---

 10 TYPES OF PEOPLE THE QUEEN SIMPLY HATES TO MEET DURING WALKABOUTS

- People who smell
- People who drop their aitches and talk like oiks
- People who want to give her a big sloppy wet kiss
- People after a hot racing tip
- People who say, 'I thought you'd be taller...' or 'Haven't you grown old?'
- Louts who want her to autograph their bottoms
- Commoners who shout 'Liz!' or 'Queenie!'
- People who want her to pose next to someone, with her arm around them
- People who say 'You look much better on the stamps...'
- People who ask her tricky questions like 'What do you think of Fergie?', 'Is Charles really loopy?' or 'Name the two stars of *Another 48 Hours*'

17 METHODS OF TRANSPORTATION THAT THE QUEEN WILL NOT NORMALLY USE TO GET TO HER PUBLIC ENGAGEMENTS

- Tube train
- 2,000 hp nitro-burning dragster
- Roller skates
- Skateboard
- Sitting astride a donkey
- Ex-NASA jet pack
- Sprinting as fast as she can
- Rickshaw
- Hitching a lift on approaches to the motorway
- No. 42 Bus
- Hang Glider
- Go-cart
- Pogo stick
- A chariot with scythes on the wheels
- Stilts
- Spacehopper
- A piggy-back from HRH Prince Philip

---

12 WOMEN WE GUARANTEE PRINCE EDWARD WILL NOT TAKE FOR HIS BRIDE

- Joan Collins
- Prunella Scales
- Jenny Powell
- Madonna
- Whitney Houston
- Enya
- Anyone from All Saints
- Dame Edna Everage
- Melinda Messenger
- Fatima Whitbread

- Paula Yates
- Anyone you know

THE ROYAL FAMILY'S 7 FAVOURITE FIZZY DRINKS

- Irn Bru (Prince Philip)
- Red Bull (The Queen Mum)
- Lucozade – blackcurrant flavour (Prince Michael of Kent)
- Pepsi Max (The Queen)
- Lilt (Viscount Linley)
- Tonic water (Princess Margaret)
- Ginger Beer (Prince Edward)

15 THINGS HER MAJESTY THE QUEEN SIMPLY CANNOT COMPREHEND

- Poverty
- Hunger
- Suffering
- Having the phone cut off
- Struggling to pay the mortgage
- Republicanism
- French kissing
- Beans on toast
- Going to work by bus
- Promotion
- Ambition
- Putting the empties out at night
- Why they let all the darkies in the country
- What Andrew ever saw in that awful blousey woman
- Labia piercing

6 THINGS PRINCE CHARLES HATES TO BE ASKED

- Are those ears real, or are you wearing them for a bet?
- Do you think you'll be too old by the time you get a shot at the throne?
- Are you completely out to lunch?
- How can you possibly fancy that Parker-Bowles?
- Why do you talk like that?
- When are you going to be king, then?

10 KINGS AND QUEENS OF ENGLAND WHO DIED STUPIDLY

- William the Conqueror – ate himself for a two-shilling bet
- King John – attempted sexual congress with a large bear
- Edward II – pulled crown on too fast and severed ears
- Henry IV – accidentally sat down on royal sceptre while naked
- Henry V – purposely sat down on royal sceptre while naked
- Elizabeth I – fell off a mountain
- George III – drowned while trying to convert the North Sea to Christianity
- George IV – green monkey disease
- William IV – caught fire while trying to light his own farts
- Victoria – auto-erotic asphyxiation

10 OTHER THINGS KING ALFRED BURNED APART FROM HIS CAKES

- His fingers (in a speculative land deal)
- His bridges (with the barons in Northumberland)
- His bra (to show solidarity with Saxon womanhood)
- Rubber (in his customised racing chariot)
- All those love letters from King Nødberg of Sweden
- His palms and his knees on the Royal Palace rug (but the less said about that, the better)
- His hair (he left the crimping tongs in the brazier for too long)
- With desire (for King Nødberg – see above)
- Witches
- The Danish flag (in an act of defiance)

---

10 REASONS TO RETAIN THE MONARCHY

- Old ladies and foreigners seem to quite like them
- They're good for a laugh
- While Princess Margaret's living in splendour, she's not living next door to you
- Someone has to defend us against the threat of being overrun by dangerous grouse, deer and foxes
- We owe it to them for inspiring a great TV show like *The Munsters*
- If the monarchy were abolished, tabloid newspapers would have no stories and would have to write about what we get up to instead and you wouldn't be able to get to your car in the

morning for all the paparazzi hanging around outside...

- Would you want their descendants in the common gene pool?
- When one of them dies, we can all have a good cry and pull together like in the Blitz blah, blah, blah, blah...
- We can all feel positively good-looking by comparison
- Comedy writers won't have anyone to take the piss out of

 ## 22 THINGS HER MAJESTY THE QUEEN WILL NEVER DO

- Win any beauty contests
- Appear as a contestant on *The Price is Right*
- A loud fart in public
- Share a bag of chips with you
- Send you a signed photograph
- Take part in an egg and spoon race
- Officially open a car-boot sale
- Get promoted
- Tell willie jokes to visiting heads of state
- Write fan letters to The Edge
- Mud wrestling
- Come round for tea
- Scratch your back for you
- Recommend a good proctologist
- Sunbathe topless in Crete
- Drink from the bottle
- Pole vault for Britain in the Olympics
- Abdicate in favour of Prince Charles
- Abdicate in favour of Richard Madely
- Wear fashionable clothes

- Play practical jokes with plastic dog turds
- Pay realistic levels of tax like the rest of us

---

 19 WORDS OR PHRASES IT WOULD BE MOST UNWISE TO USE IN CONVERSATION WITH HER MAJESTY THE QUEEN

- Plop-plops
- Spermicide jelly
- Jism
- Love blobs
- Douche
- Bum
- Strap-on
- Bonk
- Knob hound
- Euthanasia
- Colostomy bag
- Widdle
- Guff
- Crotch cheese
- Winkie
- Detumescent
- Ringpiece
- Soixante-Neuf (unless addressing Her Majesty in French and referring to that particular number)
- Kitty Kelley

 HRH PRINCE CHARLES' CLOSEST PERSONAL FRIENDS

- HRH Prince Charles
- Lady Daphne Shrub

- A bush called Henrietta
- Rodney Tulip-Bulb
- The Rt Hon. Tarquin Oak-Tree
- The Barclays Building in Shoreditch
- Lord 'Tonky' Hyacinth
- Terence Twig, The Duke of the Back Garden
- Earl Cheese Plant of Conservatory Shelf
- An eight-foot-tall blue Martian called Marmaduke

 ## SOME QUESTIONS YOU SHOULDN'T ASK IF YOU MEET HRH PRINCE PHILIP ON A WALKABOUT

- What's your favourite kebab, Phil?
- How do you reconcile being president of the World Wildlife Fund with killing animals for fun?
- Have you got change for 50p for the meter?
- Does she 'go'?
- Shot any baby animals recently?
- Come on, tell me the truth. How did you really get all those medals you're wearing?
- What's the recipe for Kleftiko?
- Was it you who just farted?
- Can you spare us a quid 'til payday, mate?
- Can you look after my dog while I pop into the supermarket for a sec?
- Would you like a salt 'n' vinegar crisp, Your Highness?

SOME GAMES YOU CAN BE SURE THE ROYALS DON'T PLAY AT SANDRINGHAM

- Hide and Seek
- Strip Poker
- Tag
- Subbuteo
- Postman's Knock
- Kiss Chase
- Arm Wrestling
- Dwarf Throwing
- Twister
- Jack the Biscuit
- Super Mario Brothers
- Spin the Bottle
- Darts

 12 THINGS THAT FERGIE WILL NEVER EVER DO
(N.B. This was a particularly hard list to compile)

- A four-minute mile
- Outsell our Rolf Harris book (ha!)
- Ask for your autograph
- Pass up a TV interview
- Pass up a bun
- Shop at Top Shop
- Cut up her credit cards
- Get back into the royal family
- Replace Diana
- Work hard
- Shut up
- Keep the weight off

Heavens above

 10 STUPID NAMES THAT ADAM AND EVE MIGHT HAVE BEEN CALLED, HAD THE BIBLE BEEN WRITTEN TODAY

- Kevin and Sharon
- Darren and Tracey
- Gary and Lisa
- Mick and Sandra
- Errol and Cath
- Martin and Angie
- Vince and Tina
- Eric and Mabel
- Steve and Elaine
- Terry and June

 1 ANIMAL THAT NOAH PROBABLY REGRETTED PUTTING IN HIS ARK

- Woodworm

 10 THINGS YOU DEFINITELY DON'T WANT TO BE REINCARNATED AS

- A tapeworm
- A dung beetle

- A tick
- Something that lives in Gordon Brown's trousers
- A backward amoeba
- A Belgian
- An Iranian girl-child
- The Boy In The Bubble
- Something that ends up in pet food
- Yourself, probably

20 OF THE MANY THINGS THAT ANGELS OF THE LORD DO NOT DO

- Organise themselves into soccer teams
- Play with themselves
- Praise The Lord with smutty little rugby ditties
- Appear when you need them
- Tell Jesus jokes
- Drink real ale
- Collect plane numbers
- Play hoopla with their halos
- Play Knock Down Ginger
- Appear on *Blind Date*
- Play 'Smack My Bitch Up' on their harps
- Play electric guitars and drums instead of harps
- Shoot up with smack
- Pinch the bottom of the angel next to them in the Choir Invisible
- Pervy things with cherubs
- Expose themselves to nuns
- Burp
- Moon passing airliners
- Fetch Indian takeaways for The Lord
- Snigger and nudge each other every time someone says, 'The coming of The Lord is nigh!'

10 STUPID SUBJECTS FOR SUNDAY SERMONS

- Bird's Eye boil-in-a-bag meals
- Julia Roberts' legs
- The life span of the emu
- *Only Fools And Horses*
- Big jobs
- Cough linctus
- Who'll be number one in the charts next week
- Key fobs
- The benefits of atheism
- Harold Pinter

 ## 10 THINGS WHICH WE HOPE THERE WON'T BE IN THE AFTERLIFE

- Cricket
- Constipation
- Bingo nights
- Folk music
- Too much religion
- Square dancing
- Babies who cry all night for ever
- Nowhere to park
- Bloody choirs everywhere
- Benny Hill in cabaret – every night for eternity

---

12 THINGS WHICH WE HOPE THERE WILL BE IN THE AFTERLIFE

- Sex
- Bell's Whisky
- Juke Boxes (and change for them)
- Ferrari F40s for everyone

- Raucous parties that you don't remember a thing about the epoch after
- A branch of Nationwide (so we *can* take it with us...)
- Comfy beds
- Kinky underwear
- Blondes
- Pubs
- Cream cakes made of manna with no calories
- Amazonian women who just won't take no for an answer

---

11 THINGS THAT GOD FROWNS UPON YOU PRAYING FOR

- £1 million in untraceable used notes
- Alicia Silverstone and a vat of semolina
- Four extra inches
- The Spice Girls' tour bus to be in simultaneous collision with six petrol tankers and a lorry carrying high explosives
- A new Masserati
- A Rolex
- The off-licence still to be open
- Fine weather for the second test
- A large tax error in your favour
- Unimaginable violence descending upon your boss
- Proof

🐸 10 STUPID WAYS TO TRY TO TRICK YOUR WAY THROUGH THE PEARLY GATES, IF ST PETER REFUSES TO LET YOU IN

- Avon calling!
- A package for Mr God...
- Jehovah's Witnesses! (They'll pretend to be out)
- I've come to read the meter...
- Is this the party? I'm a mate of John's...
- I'm a vet. I hear you've got an angel in there with wing moult...
- I'm from the local council. We're doing this survey...
- My car's broken down. Can I use your phone, please?
- I've come to give the cherabim their singing lessons
- I'm a television talent scout, come to audition the choir invisible...

🐛 28 ENTERTAINERS NAMED AFTER CHARACTERS IN THE BIBLE

- MADONNA
- Chris ISAAK
- ESTHER Rantzen
- MARY Hopkin
- David JACOBs
- JOSEPH Bottoms
- JESSE Matthews
- MARK Lamarr
- MIRIAM Karlin
- JOHN Fashanu
- LUKE Perry
- MATTHEW Kelly

- PAUL Young
- SARAH Brightman
- MICHAEL CAINe
- BENJAMIN Britten
- DEBORAH Harry
- DANIEL Day-Lewis
- Father ABRAHAM and the Smurfs
- RUTH Maddock
- ADAM West
- JONATHAN Ross
- EVE Graham (of 'New Seekers' fame)
- Peter GABRIEL
- DAVID Essex
- RACHEL Ward
- Yannick NOAH (A tennis player, apparently)
- GODley & Creme

11 OCCASIONS ON WHICH YOU DON'T WANT THE VIRGIN MARY SUDDENLY TO APPEAR UNTO YOU

- While walking a tightrope over Niagara Falls
- During your psychiatric evaluation
- Just when you're trying to convince your wife that you haven't got another woman in the house
- Just as you're about to bring your jumbo jet in to land at Heathrow
- While indulging in a furtive wank
- Just *after* you've given the Pope the finger
- Just as you're in the process of applying some Preparation H...
- When you're shaving off your pubic hair with a cutthroat razor
- While attempting to summon up the devil

- While dressing up in your wife's clothes and parading up and down in front of the mirror
- While interfering with barnyard fowl

---

12 STUPID PLACES FOR THE SECOND COMING TO OCCUR

- On the moon
- Outside Burger King
- Inside Britain's largest mental hospital
- Between two slices of bread
- Inside a small septic tank
- Behind your skirting board
- At a midnight showing of *Life of Brian*
- In your bedroom just when you're trying to get to sleep
- In a patch of quicksand
- In the fast lane of the M1
- Glasgow on a Saturday night
- Milton Keynes (any time)

---

10 THINGS WHICH THE BIBLE FAILS TO GIVE US ANY GUIDANCE ON

- If Adam and Eve were the first people, then who did Cain marry?
- Who was God's dad?
- Why do we always seem to get cramp at that vital moment?
- How to be an incredible lover
- Who's the better singer – Whitney Houston or Janet Jackson?
- Making quiche Lorraine
- What to make of Janet Street Porter

- Why there is a Birmingham
- How to get a recording contract
- Does Utterley Butterly really taste like butter?

9 NAMES YOU WON'T FIND IN THE OLD TESTAMENT

- Cosmo
- Wendy
- Godzilla
- Bob
- Great Uncle Bulgaria
- Fatty
- Po
- Waynetta
- Jesus

11 GIFTS THAT THE BABY JESUS PROBABLY WOULD HAVE WANTED INSTEAD OF GOLD, FRANKINCENSE AND MYRRH IF HE WERE ALIVE TODAY

- Nintendo 64
- Walkman with auto reverse and a three-band graphic equaliser
- Mountain bike
- Walkie Talkie set
- Radio-controlled model jeep
- £30 record token
- Digital camcorder
- Tasty trainers
- Set of all the *Alien* videos
- Laptop computer
- 'Le Mans' Scalextric set

10 THINGS IT'S STUPID TO CLAIM JESUS EVER SAID

- 'Whose round is it?'
- 'It's my Monopoly set so I'll be the car!'
- 'Will you marry me?'
- 'Big Mac and large fries, please'
- 'Come on you Spurs!'
- 'I've seen *Star Wars* ten times'
- 'You're going home in an ambulance'
- 'Sorted!'
- 'My mate fancies you...'
- 'You don't get many of those to the pound, love!'

10 STUPID THINGS THAT NUNS NEVER DO

- Hold 'Who's Got The Biggest Bosoms' contests
- Drink eight cans of Special Brew after lights out
- Read dirty mags
- Arm wrestle for money
- Arm wrestle for the hell of it
- Take it in turns to have wild sex with the gardener behind the potting shed
- Blaspheme using sign language
- Wear open-crotch panties and red silk basques
- Get tattooed
- Press-ups in the cucumber patch (despite the rumours)

12 PLAGUES THAT MOSES COULD HAVE SMITTEN THE EGYPTIANS WITH

- The plague of hair on the palms of your hands so that people look at you funny
- The plague of the first born destined to grow up to become hairdressers and choreographers
- The plague of crocodiles nesting in your girdle
- The plague of being right next door to Libya
- The plague of beautiful maidens who are only interested in your money
- The plague of just missing the chariot to work and having to wait half an hour for the next one to come along
- The plague of running out of eggs just when you really fancy an omelette
- The plague of itchy groins in public
- The plague of head colds that just won't go away, no matter how much orange juice you drink
- The plague of hair that you can't do a thing with
- The plague of not being able to get a date on Friday night
- The plague of forty-foot pubic lice

14 THINGS IT WOULD BE VERY STUPID FOR THE POPE TO DO

- Walk around with a huge black panther straining at the leash
- Snigger every time he says 'You may kiss my ring'
- Hit himself on the head with a mallet
- Do wheelies on a top-of-the-range Harley

- Get someone pregnant
- Rip all his clothes off and run shrieking through St Peter's
- Record a duet with Madonna
- Come out of the closet
- Tell everyone it's all been a big hoax...
- Declare that, henceforth, he wishes to be known as 'Lucille'
- Drive the Popemobile in a demolition derby
- Appear in a Durex commercial
- Lose his faith
- Use the Turin Shroud to wipe his bottom

10 HEADLINES YOU'RE EXTREMELY UNLIKELY TO SEE IN 'THE WAR CRY'

- WAS JESUS A SPACE ALIEN?
- HOLY TRINITY IN BIZARRE LOVE TRIANGLE
- 5000 CANS OF SPECIAL BREW MUST BE WON INSIDE!
- MALE SALVATIONIST GIVES BIRTH TO TWO-HEADED ALIEN BABY
- LIMBLESS MISSIONARY MARRIES AFRICAN PYGMY CONVERT!
- WAS WILLIAM BOOTH A WOMAN?
- HEAVEN FOUND – IN ILFORD!
- SALVATION ARMY MARCHING BAND FOUND ON MARS!
- IT'S OFFICIAL! SALLY ARMY CAPTAINS MAKE BETTER LOVERS!
- INSIDE: PLAY 'SPOT THE SINNER'...AND WIN, WIN, WIN!

10 STUPID THINGS TO GIVE UP FOR LENT

- Breathing
- Your religious beliefs
- Fellatio
- Incredible wealth
- Fast cars
- Well-endowed women
- Jaffa cakes
- Getting a seat on crowded trains
- Staying up late watching dirty videos and drinking beer with the lads
- Going to the toilet

 10 SENSIBLE THINGS TO GIVE UP FOR LENT

- Venture scouting
- Paying tax, national insurance and VAT
- Chastity
- Sex with marsupials
- Watching Jim Davidson's *Big Break*
- Spice Girls albums
- Train spotting
- Alimony payments
- Going to the dentist
- Having anything whatsoever to do with lawyers

 10 STUPID NAMES FOR SALVATION ARMY SOUP KITCHENS WHICH WANT TO APPEAR CHIC

- Hobo's
- Bumms of Covent Garden

- Wino's
- The Little Tramp
- Dossers of Berwick Street
- Monsieur Vagrant
- Dine 'n' Out
- The Hard Luck Cafe
- Itinerenti
- Chez Box

---

 10 STUPID THINGS YOU NEVER SEE PEOPLE DO IN *SONGS OF PRAISE*

- Proudly hold a burning cross
- Sing rude words to the tune of 'Jerusalem'
- Read unsavoury literature hidden behind their hymn books
- Fart to the tune 'He Who Would Valiant Be'
- Pick their nose and flick it
- Wear a goat's head mask
- Look as though they're having a really good time
- Wave at the camera and do V-signs behind the head of the person sitting in the pew in front
- Hold up a placard saying 'Hello Heavenly Father'
- Look younger than seventy

Culture shock

🎵 **14 STUPID FILMS THAT COMBINE THE THRILLS OF GARDENING AND WAR**

- *A Greenhouse Too Far*
- *Apocalypse Patio*
- *Trellis Over The River Kwai*
- *The Blue Trug*
- *The Mulch Of Iwo Jima*
- *The Heroes Of The Garden Centre*
- *Hoe Of Iron*
- *The Hosepipe Ban Of Navarone*
- *Flora! Flora! Flora!*
- *Von Ryan's Shrub*
- *The Longest Hardy Perennial*
- *633 Sprinkler*
- *F*O*R*K*
- *Sink The Dahlia*

---

 10 NICKNAMES FOR COMEDIANS IF THEY WERE AS FAT AS ROY 'CHUBBY' BROWN

- Woody 'Lard Arse' Allen
- Harry 'Gut Bucket' Hill
- Steve 'Michelin Man' Martin
- Lee 'Meatloaf' Hurst
- Billy 'Porker' Crystal

- Jack 'Fat Bastard' Dee
- Ben 'Fatso' Elton
- Robin 'Fatty Arbuckle' Williams
- David 'Bernard Manning' Baddiel
- Jim 'Looks Like Ten Pounds Of Shit In A Five-Pound Bag' Davidson

---

12 UNSUITABLE PERFORMERS TO ENTERTAIN THE FRAIL AND ELDERLY

- Eric and His Pyrotechnics Par Excellence
- Mr Harwood and His Daredevil Stunt Kittens
- Leather Marion's Bondage Half-Hour
- The Sudden Loud Noise Experience
- DJ Ranking Leroy B's 40 Megawatt Sound System
- The Nudie Royal Lookalikes Show
- Sonia The Viper Juggler and Bill
- The Nottingham Slam Dancers (audience participation encouraged)
- The Tyrolean Blindfolded Yodelling Tumblers
- Billy Jenkins' Horror Roadshow
- The Lash Brothers' Whipcrackaway Wild West Show
- Danny Tib's Dying-Animal Impressions Show

---

7 PREDICTABLE SEQUELS TO *THE COLOUR PURPLE*

- *The Colour Orange*
- *The Colour Crimson*
- *The Colour Brown*
- *The Colour Yellow*
- *The Colour Aquamarine*
- *The Colour Puce*
- *The Colour Purple II*

10 STUPID REASONS THE TELETUBBIES MIGHT SPLIT UP

- Laa-Laa decides to go solo
- Tinky Winky is found hanged by a belt in his hotel room
- Frustration after contractual wrangles prevent them from releasing a follow-up single to 'Say Eh-Oh'
- Dipsy and Po die from eating salmonella-infected Tubby custard
- Tinky Winky is forced into rehab to curb his methadone addiction
- Dipsy finds religion and joins a mysterious Eastern cult
- A scandal involving Mr Blobby, the Bananas in Pyjamas and a Class 'A' drug
- Tinky Winky, Laa-Laa and Po are shot dead in a vicious revenge attack by an embittered Bungle
- Po is burned beyond all recognition in a tragic Tubby toast accident
- 'Artistic differences'

11 STUPID WAYS TO TRY TO COMMUNICATE THE PHILOSOPHY OF SOCRATES TO THE GENERAL PUBLIC

- An ice-show spectacular
- A weekly sitcom
- Mime
- As an encrypted computer file
- Semaphore
- As a series of complicated anagrams
- In skywriting
- Using the Teletubbies or the Bananas in Pyjamas

- Subliminally, during episodes of *London's Burning*
- As a daily strip cartoon in the *Sun*
- Written on a small piece of paper hidden down your trousers

---

♫ 6 STUPID PREVIOUS WORKING TITLES TO PRINCE'S HIT 'RASPBERRY BERET'

- 'Blackberry Fedora'
- 'Loganberry Fez'
- 'Strawberry Stetson'
- 'Blueberry Trilby'
- 'Elderberry Panama'
- 'Raspberry That Sort Of Flat Hat That The Frenchies All Wear, You Know, Like A Pancake. Shit! Why Can't I Remember The Damn Name?'

 ## 10 FILMS YOU'RE UNLIKELY TO SEE ARNOLD SCHWARZENEGGER IN

- The Love That Dared Not Speak Its Name
- Rosie and Jim's Canal-Boat Holiday Adventure
- Dormitory Sluts
- Carry on Knitting
- Anything that casts him as a dwarf
- Or a committed coprophiliac
- Or someone with an impeccable English accent
- A remake of *The Wizard of Oz* – with him as Dorothy
- Anything where he gets second billing to Dolph Lundgren
- Anything with the words 'Dialectic' or 'Semiotic Theory' in the title

10 WORDS TOP POETS FEAR AND DREAD (BECAUSE THEY'RE DIFFICULT TO RHYME)

- Rhythm
- Commensurate
- Antidisestablishmentarianism
- Llandudno
- Corkscrew
- Anomaly
- Gorgonzola
- Sulphide
- Misapprehension
- Phlegm

---

1 WORD TOP POETS FEAR AND DREAD (PARTICULARLY WHEN IT FALLS AT THE END OF A LINE)

- Venus

THE 11 LEAST SUCCESSFUL CIRCUS ACTS OF ALL TIME

- Phlegmo, the spitting clown and Hawky
- 'Wobbly' Franco, the one-legged stilt walker
- Eddie 'Mr Vertigo' Kopecnik, high-wire dancer
- Imogen 'clean shaven' Futtock, the bearded lady
- Zachary the so-so, the myopic knife-thrower
- Stella and Renaldo, amputee jugglers
- Captain Jack and his troupe of performing plankton
- 'Scaredy Cat' Peterson, lion tamer
- Fatty Hamilton, human cannonball
- Harry 'Claustrophobic' Hall, escapologist

• 'Hernia' Stromboli, the world's strongest man

11 STUPID BITS OF A BOOK THAT NOBODY GIVES A TOSS ABOUT

• Where it was printed
• The recommended price in New Zealand
• The number above the bar code
• The number below the bar code
• The bar code
• The address of the publisher
• The introduction
• Who the authors want to thank
• Who designed the front cover
• The bit that starts 'This book is sold subject to the condition...'
• 99% of the content

6 ALTERNATIVE NAMES FOR 'MAN FRIDAY' IF ROBINSON CRUSOE HAD FOUND HIM ON A DIFFERENT DAY

• Man Monday
• Man Saturday
• Man Thursday
• Man Sunday
• Man Wednesday
• Man Tuesday

13 STUPID THINGS TO ATTEMPT TO TAKE WITH YOU INTO THE NATIONAL GALLERY

• A flame-thrower

- A large Gurkha knife
- An armoured vehicle
- A bag marked 'swag'
- A spray can and stencil
- A bucket of fresh dung and a catapult
- A frenzied Rottweiler
- A huge glass tank filled with ultra-destructive Death's-head moths
- Yourself, stark-naked, except for a strap-on dildo attached to your forehead
- A party of epileptics, each carrying a brand new set of ginsu knives
- A large sheet of tracing paper and a stepladder
- A larger container of industrial-strength paint stripper and a scraper
- A hammer and chisel in a bag marked 'Acme Statue Improvement Service'

---

 10 STUPID THINGS TO ATTEMPT TO TAKE OUT OF THE NATIONAL GALLERY

- The piss
- One of the curators in a sack
- A wild animal (they haven't got any)
- The cloakroom
- The frame of the most valuable painting on display
- A busty art student in a sack
- The foundations
- A cup of tea from the cafeteria, balanced on your head
- The floors
- *In The Park* by Claude Monet (it's in the Tate, stupid!)

♪ ♫ 10 STUPID REASONS WHY 'THE DEVIL HAS ALL THE BEST TUNES'

- You can't dance to harp music
- There's a branch of HMV in Hell
- God had some good records, but they got stolen
- He's younger than God and more 'with it'
- God is tone deaf
- The devil has more disposable income to spend on luxuries like CDs
- He never lends his records to friends who don't return them
- Rave music is banned in Hell
- The devil got Jim Morrison. God got Jim Reeves
- Jesus likes Bluegrass

---

10 STORYLINES YOU'LL NEVER SEE IN *CORONATION STREET* (UNLESS COMPETITION FROM *EASTENDERS* IS PARTICULARLY INTENSE)

- Emily Bishop discovers she's three months pregnant but who's the father? Chief suspects are Jack Duckworth and Kevin Webster
- Roy Battersby and Gail have a torrid affair, part of which includes them acting out his strange fantasies involving jelly and power tools
- Brian Tilsley comes back from the dead as a blood-crazed zombie who hideously disfigures Deirdre, although no one notices for five episodes
- In an unsurpassed declaration of brotherly devotion, Steve and Andy Macdonald decide to become Siamese twins

- Maud Grimes, under the influence of a possessed packet of fish fingers, hacks Alma Baldwin into bits with a machete and hides her body in the deep freeze
- Audrey Roberts has a torrid lesbian affair with Janice Battersby
- Mike Baldwin jacks in his job and sells all his wordly goods to become a simple travelling troubadour
- Des Barnes tries to commit suicide by taking an overdose of Junior Disprin after a lovers' spat with Ken Barlow
- Vera Duckworth, Maxine and Liz Macdonald join a strange religious sect that preaches bestiality
- Curly Watts has a vegetable duel with Nick Tilsley for the affection of Leanne Battersby and sustains life-threatening injuries from a lettuce

10 THINGS THAT VINCENT VAN GOGH COULDN'T DO

- Count up to two, using his ears
- Make full use of a Sony Walkman
- Keep more than one paintbrush behind his ears
- Wear a pair of sunglasses and keep them straight
- Wear a pair of matching stud earrings
- Impersonate someone with two ears
- Have the nickname 'Dumbo'
- Put his hand on his heart and say that he never once mutilated his head
- Grin from ear to ear
- Tell if something was in stereo

🎵 **10 STUPID THINGS THAT LEONARDO DA VINCI COULD HAVE BEEN DOING IN ORDER TO MAKE THE MONA LISA SMILE**

- Opening and closing his flies in time to music
- Doing his impression of Michelangelo pissed
- Telling the one about Pope Julius II, the goat and the lasagne
- Demonstrating a prototype clockwork vibrator that he'd just invented
- Telling her that, one day, heavier-than-air flight would be possible
- A big wet juicy fart
- Saying that one day this painting would be hanging in the Louvre – which she misheard as 'loo'
- Painting, unaware that he had a big blob of green paint on his chin
- Tickling her nether regions with a long feather duster
- Telling her he was going to pay her ten times more than he actually was

 1 CURRENT NEWSPAPER NAMED AFTER SOMETHING WITH AN INTERNAL TEMPERATURE OF 35,000,000° C.

- The *Sun*

 1 DEFUNCT NEWSPAPER NAMED AFTER THE PLANET VENUS

- The *Morning Star*

🎵 9 PSYCHOLOGICAL THRILLERS ABOUT STAMP COLLECTING

- *Fatal Collection*
- *Whatever Happened To Stanley Gibbons?*
- *The 1856 British Guyana One-Cent Magenta Vanishes*
- *The Thirty-Nine Tweezers*
- *Strangers on a First Day Cover*
- *Mint Instinct*
- *North by North Philately*
- *Psycho Penny Black*
- *The Jagged Edge (aka Perforation)*

THE NUMBER OF BUTTOCKS POSSESSED BY 10 PROMINENT ARTISTS

- David Hockney (Two)
- Sandro Botticelli (Two)
- Jackson Pollock (Two)
- Albrecht Durer (Two)
- Ford Madox Brown (Two)
- Hans the Younger Holbein (Two)
- Marc Chagall (Two)
- Auguste Renoir (Two)
- Edvard Munch (Two)
- Salvador Dali (Fish)